THE INSIDER'S
ATLANTA
A METROPOLITAN
RESOURCE BOOK

By Philippa Maister
Illustrations by Thomas Hogan

GOOD·HOPE·PRESS

Published by
GOOD HOPE PRESS
75 Silverwood Road, N. E.
Atlanta, Georgia 30342

Copyright© 1982 Philippa Maister Ahuja

Cover photograph: Kiyoaki Kato
Cover design: Debbie Feldman
Typography: Betty and Becky Adams
Pasteup: Jo-Anne Friedlander

Cover: Ansley Park

First edition, first printing

ISBN 0-9608596-0-8

For

KRISH

who supported,
encouraged,
and endured,

and for

VINITA.

The author owes a great debt of gratitude to literally scores of individuals who took the time to provide facts, grant background interviews, or suggest items that have been incorporated into the fabric of this book. Needless to say, they are not responsible for any errors.

This book is as accurate as painstaking research and careful checking and rechecking can make it. Nevertheless, time brings change. So we suggest you make use of the phone numbers provided to ensure that the addresses, days, and hours of opening listed still hold.

It is our hope to update this volume regularly to keep abreast of the continuing growth of Atlanta. The author would welcome information about new developments, or items of interest inadvertently omitted from this book, for inclusion in later editions.

No consideration of any kind has been received for mention of any organization or business on these pages.

Milking Rosebud, Mathis Dairy

CONTENTS

III. GETTING AROUND

IV. LEARNING EXPERIENCES

V. CULTURAL AFFAIRS

VI. GOOD TIMES

VII. PRINT & PRATTLE: The Media In Atlanta

VIII. HEY, BIG SPENDERS!

IX. FOOD, GLORIOUS FOOD

X. THE OUTDOORS AT YOUR DOORSTEP

"Out in the Rain." Oakland Cemetery

INTRODUCING ATLANTA

If you take the glass-fronted elevator to the top of the Peachtree Plaza Hotel downtown and while away an hour in the restaurant there, watching the city slowly revolve about you, the chief features of Atlanta will become clear.

Perhaps the first thing that will strike you is that the tall buildings of the downtown area are like an island in a sea of forest. Viewed from above, the vast metropolis is like an invisible city, and its residents like it that way. They like their buildings low and shaded by trees. The city even employs an arborist to protect its trees against the ravages of excessive development. Atlanta is a pretty city, and in the spring, when white clouds of dogwood line the streets, it's like a dream.

If you follow the line of tall buildings to the north, you'll observe the course of Peachtree Street, the central thoroughfare of the city. Peachtree Street begins just south of your vantage point, at Five Points, where Atlanta itself began.

Just to the south of the downtown area lies the drab inner city; like most other large cities, Atlanta has pockets of poverty with poor housing and high unemployment. To the east, close in, many of the city's older neighborhoods are experiencing a revival as young professionals move in and renovate. Further out, bounding the city on all sides, lie the comfortable neighborhoods of Atlanta's Black and White middle classes.

Beyond the city, stretching out in every direction, lies the metropolitan area. For Atlanta is both a city and a region. Atlanta, the city, is at the core, occupying most of Fulton County and part of DeKalb. Atlanta, the region, occupies seven counties (Clayton, Cobb, DeKalb, Douglas, Fulton, Gwinnett and Rockdale) for planning purposes, and 15 (the above plus Butts, Cherokee, Forsyth, Henry, Fayette, Newton, Paulding, and Walton) for statistical pur-

1

poses. These 15 constitute the Atlanta Standard Metropolitan Statistical Area (SMSA).

Suburbia is steadily encroaching on the rural areas surrounding the city proper, keeping pace with the swift expansion of the regional economy which brings an estimated 30,000 newcomers to Atlanta every year.

The People of Atlanta

When you descend from your lookout point to mingle with the people in the streets, you'll find a city bustling with persons from all parts of the United States and other countries — yet one that retains many of its Southern qualities.

It's a city in which convention, material comfort, and leisure are highly valued. The daughters of old White families of distinguished pedigree still make their debuts in Society on the arms of their fathers, with a curtsey at formal balls. The rural dances of the South flourish too, and clogging — perhaps a precursor of tap — is enjoying a revival in Atlanta. Religion is a vital element in the social fabric; churches abound, and are full on Sundays. Y'all is really said here, as in, "Y'all come back and see us." And $3.50 will still buy you a plate of fried chicken, collard greens, blackeyed peas, and cornbread muffins in some of the city's cafeterias.

A distinctive feature of Atlanta is the long history, size, and wealth of its Black middle class. As early as 1859, Atlanta's first Black dentist, Roderick D. Badger, set up an extensive Black and White practice in the city. Another Atlantan, Henry Flipper, became the first Black to graduate from West Point in 1877. In 1905, Alonzo F. Herndon established an insurance company, Atlanta Life, which has grown to be one of the largest Black enterprises in the nation. And, of course, Atlanta was the birthplace of Dr. Martin Luther King, Jr.

Today, native Atlantans are greatly outnumbered by migrants drawn to the city for many reasons. Some are refugees from the cold and blustery winters of the North. But Atlanta also has a surprising diversity of ethnic groups from all over the world.

Perhaps the largest single group in this category is Spanish-speaking. Slightly over half the Spanish-speaking population is of Cuban origin. The rest are mainly from Mexico, Puerto Rico, Colombia, and other South American nations. They celebrate their culture each year in Atlanta during National Hispanic Heritage Week.

Another popular festival is hosted by the city's Greek community at their beautiful Cathedral of the Annunciation with its magnificent mosaics. The Goethe Institute and its many free cultural programs testify to the German presence here. Atlanta's Chinese, Korean, Indo-Chinese, Indian, and Middle Eastern populations add Oriental spice to the region. In fact, scores of social clubs have been formed by members of these and other nationalities; you'll find a list in *"Atlanta: A Guide for International Visitors,"* available from the Atlanta

Convention and Visitors Bureau.

So, while Atlanta is still a "Southern" city, the seeds of cosmopolitan diversity are beginning to germinate. Atlanta is not a city for radicals, but it does tolerate a range of opinion varying from far right to just left of center. And it boasts a variety of cultural, intellectual, and just plain fun things to do.

This book will lead you to them.

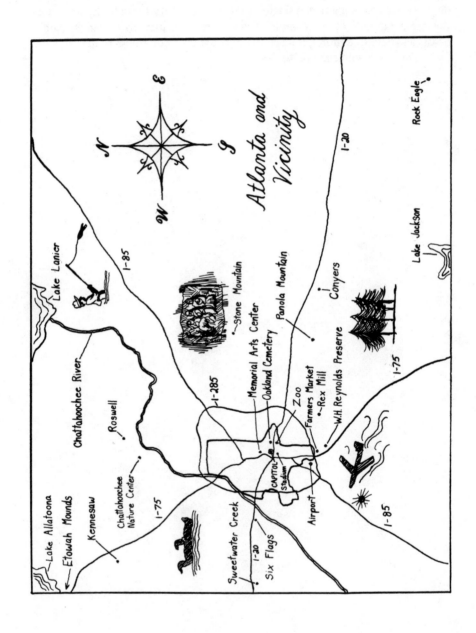

I

WHAT'S WHAT

The Lion of Atlanta, Oakland Cemetery

HOW
ATLANTA
GREW

The reason Atlanta was founded is the reason it continues to grow: its location. The city was barely 20 years old when its citizens were describing it as the "Gate-City of the South." They chose this title for the city, according to one account, "because it stands at the meeting of the roads that lead down along the mountainsides from the north and up along the river banks from the south, and opens its doors both ways for the intercommunications of the people."

The Birth of Atlanta

Atlanta got its start in 1837, when a site near the present Five Points was chosen as the eastern end of the Western and Atlantic Railroad. This spot was dubbed Terminus. The name, it was dryly said, "for several years expressed all that was significant in the place."

In 1840, six families had Terminus to themselves. But by 1850, five years after the inauguration of the first regular rail service from Augusta, the population had grown to 3,000. Terminus, now the junction of three railroads, had already outgrown its name; in 1843 it was renamed Marthasville, after the daughter of the then governor Wilson Lumpkin. In 1845, a flight of fancy converted the town into Atlanta. The name, a writer commented, "typified the Atlantic ocean, conveying the impression of greatness and movement that so marked the new city. It was to become a place as deep and broad as the great ocean."

The Righteous Vs. The Riotous

The city incorporated in 1847 had all the characteristics of a frontier

7

town. With one liquor store for every 60 inhabitants, "there was a reign of whisky and of violence; there was a constant defiance of law; there was disorder, fighting and rioting." What was needed was a strong man. He emerged in the form of Mayor Jonathan Norcross. In the elections of 1850, Norcross's Moral Party wooed the voters with confectionery and apples while the Rowdy Party seduced them with liquor. Beaten at the polls, the Rowdies made a last stand in the streets. But they were dispersed by 600 armed-to-the-teeth supporters of Mayor Norcross. From this time on, Atlanta was free to pursue its primary interest: trade.

In 1860, as the city stood on the brink of war, Atlanta had more than quadrupled its population to 13,000. Elegant three-story brick residences lined the main streets. Trade, boosted by the high price of cotton, was thriving. But the rumblings of war were clearly audible.

The Civil War

Ignoring the warnings of some of its citizens, the city threw in its lot with that of the rest of the South. So Atlanta went to war, its railroads and industrial might making it a powerful military center of the Confederacy. There was a rush of volunteers to join the Confederate Army.

But valor alone could not produce the victory. The Union Army, under Sherman, pressed on into the South, with Atlanta a prime target. In July 1864, federal forces began drawing the net tighter round the city, aided, inadvertently, by the Confederates' decision to change generals in mid-campaign. As Confederate soldiers fought desperately on Atlanta's borders to save the city, the city itself suffered continual bombardment by Sherman's cannons. Refugees began to stream southward out of Atlanta.

By the end of August, Atlanta was surrounded. The Confederates were forced to withdraw, blowing up 70 carloads of powder and shells as they left to prevent them falling into Yankee hands. In the process, many of the city's houses were destroyed. The Mayor and City Council surrendered to Sherman, who ordered the city evacuated. In November, Sherman, preparing for his March to the Sea at Savannah, ordered that Atlanta's industrial and railroad plant, its public buildings and warehouses be put to the torch to destroy the city's value as a military base. The combined effect of the shelling, Hood's actions and Sherman's orders was devastating: of Atlanta's 3,800 houses, only about 400 survived.

The Phoenix City

Within a month, however, Atlanta's inhabitants began to return to their city and rebuild. By 1870, the city's population had risen to 22,000.

Small wonder then that Atlanta's citizens chose as the symbol of their city the Phoenix, the mythical bird of the Arabian desert that, every 600 years, burnt itself on a funeral pile to rise from the ashes with renewed youth.

By 1895, with a population of some 80,000, Atlanta was ready to show itself off to the rest of the world by means of the great Cotton States and International Exposition, held in what is now Piedmont Park. The city was just emerging from a severe recession, and the Exposition was designed both to display the strengths of Atlanta's economy — to show, as Henry Grady, editor of *The Atlanta Constitution,* had put it earlier, that "the South has been rebuilt by Southern brains and energy" — and to attract Northern investment to the South. Symbolically, a Black man, Booker T. Washington, was invited to be one of the speakers at the opening day.

Post-Bellum Atlanta

Since the Civil War, Atlanta has not allowed ideology to override pragmatic self-interest. You could almost describe the city's motto as "Make deals, not war."

This is not to say that racial tensions have not surfaced. They have. In 1906, a race riot divided the city. Segregation was made law when Reconstruction ended. In general, however, Atlantans have accepted change once they have seen the writing on the wall.

Thus, in the 1960's, when Black students used sit-ins, shop-ins, and other devices to force an end to racial segregation in stores, restaurants, and public places in Atlanta, they were able to achieve peaceful desegregation within four years. Business, said the city's leaders, let's get back to business.

The recent history of Atlanta has been one of economic expansion and population growth, some within the city limits, much in neighboring counties. And the prognosis for the future is more of the same.

"Atlanta," says the Chamber of Commerce enthusiastically, "A city without limits."

For Further Reading

– – – –	*Atlanta Centennial, 1837-1937* (Atlanta: G. Murphy, n.d.)
– – – –	*Atlanta Resurgens* (Atlanta: First National Bank of Atlanta, 1971)
– – – –	*City of Atlanta* (Louisville: Interstate Publishing Co., 1892-1893)
George Leonard Chaney	*The New South – Atlanta*
Franklin M. Garrett	*Atlanta and Environs* (Athens: University of Georgia Press, 1969)

9

Martin Luther King, Junior
1929-1968

Martin Luther King, Jr. is undoubtedly Atlanta's most famous son.

Born at 501 Auburn Avenue, Dr. King was to become a symbol throughout the world of the power of nonviolent action in bringing about social reform. His leadership of the American civil rights movement from 1955 until his death was instrumental in bringing about profound social change in a racially-divided nation, and in forever ending segregation in the South. Among many honors, Dr. King was awarded the Nobel Peace Prize in 1964. On April 4, 1968, he was killed by an assassin's bullet in Memphis, Tennessee.

An eternal flame burns beside Dr. King's grave in Auburn Avenue, near the place where he was born. A simple inscription on his tomb, taken from one of his most famous speeches, reads: *"Free at last, free at last, thank God almighty, I'm free at last."*

In 1980, Congress designated part of Auburn Avenue the Martin Lurther King Jr. National Historic Site in order "to protect and interpret for the benefit, inspiration, and education of present and future generations the places where Martin Luther King, Junior, was born, where he lived, worked, and worshipped, and where he is buried."

THE
INDIAN
PAST

Long, long ago, before there was an Atlanta or a Terminus, before there were colonists, or Creeks, or Cherokees, before Ericsson sailed to Vinland, men roamed these hills. They left relics of their presence as small as arrowheads and as tall as five-story buildings.

At Allatoona, just north of the modern Atlanta, archaeologists have found sites occupied by nomadic spearhunters 10,000 years before the birth of Christ.

Soapstone Ridge in DeKalb County reveals the impact of men who worked its stone deposits between 4000 and 1000 B.C. From the soft but heat-resistant rock they chipped out chunks, then shaped them into bowls and cooking-pots with wooden mallets and chisels made from deer antlers. Boulders still show the marks of this activity.

Between 1000 B.C. and 800 A.D., agricultural, pottery-making communities settled near Atlanta. They left magnificent evidence of their presence at **Rock Eagle** near Eatonton, some 120 miles east of Atlanta. Used for religious ceremonies, this giant effigy of an eagle was built between 1000 B.C. and 200 A.D. from quartz rocks carried to the site, probably, by hand. It measures 102 feet from crown to tail, 120 feet from wingtip to wingtip, and sits 10 feet below ground, 10 feet above. The structure can be viewed from an observation tower during daylight hours.

During the Mississippian period (800-1540 A.D.), Indian villages were settled along the Chattahoochee. These matrilineal communities were headed by priest-chiefs and traded extensively with distant regions, using a well-developed network of trails.

The **Etowah Mounds** south of Cartersville were constructed during this period, within a fortified town which served as a ceremonial center for the region. Atop these mounds, the largest of which stood 53 feet high and occupied several acres, were built temples and mortuary houses of the chiefs. Elaborate ceremonial objects, including marble figurines and copper ornaments, have been found at Etowah. The site and museum, off Ga. 61, are open to the public Tuesday through Saturday from 9 a.m. to 5 p.m. and Sunday from 2 to 5:30 p.m. (tel.: 1-382-2704).

Other structures dating from this period are the Ocmulgee National Monument near Macon, and the Kolomoki Mounds near Blakely.

Creeks and Cherokees

The year 1540 saw the arrival of the first Europeans under Hernando DeSoto, bringing with them war and diseases that decimated Indian populations. Survivors grouped themselves into nations such as the Creeks, whose domain was roughly south of the Chattahoochee, and the Cherokees, who lived north of it.

Gradually, White settlement robbed the Indians of most of their lands, intensifying in the late 18th and early 19th centuries. Not even "civilization" could save them.

The Cherokees tried it, under their leader Sequoya, who developed a Cherokee alphabet in 1821. Within months his people had achieved widespread literacy. By 1828, at their capital in New Echota, they were publishing a weekly newspaper of their own, "The Cherokee Phenix."

But this phoenix signalled no rebirth, especially after gold was discovered in Dahlonega.

Between 1836 and 1840, 20,000 Creeks were forced to march to Oklahoma for resettlement. In the winter of 1838 and 1839, the same fate befell the 14,000 Cherokees, about one-quarter of whom died on what was to be known as "The Trail of Tears."

The event is commemorated each year from June through August in Cherokee, North Carolina in a dramatic production called, "Unto These Hills." It is performed by descendants of the 1,000 Cherokees who escaped the exile by fleeing into the Great Smoky Mountains, and were later granted a small reservation there.

For Further Reading

Roy S. Dickens Jr. & James L. McKinley	*Frontiers in the Soil: The Archaeology of Georgia* (Atlanta: Frontiers Publishing Co., 1979)
Georgia Office of Indian Heritage	"Georgia's Major Historic Indian Sites" and "Indian Trails of Georgia."
Frederick W. Hodge	*Handbook of American Indians North of Mexico,* Parts I and II (New Jersey: Rownan and Littlefield, 1979)
Thomas M. N. Lewis & Madeline Kneberg	*Tribes That Slumber* (Knoxville: University of Tennessee Press, 1977)

Atlanta's Time Capsule

Buried beneath the Oglethorpe University campus under two feet of bedrock, protected by porcelain embedded in pitch, and sealed with a great steel door welded shut, lies the Crypt of Civilization.

No man may look on its contents until the year 8113. But we know what they are: a record of man's past 6,000 years.

The Crypt was the brainchild of Dr. Thornwell Jacobs, who was president of Oglethorpe from 1913 to 1944. He conceived the idea in 1935 when his own researches into ancient civilizations were being hampered by lack of accurate information. Dr. Jacobs resolved that historians of the future should be spared such ignorance about our own civilization. In August 1937, with the aid of a scientist, Thomas K. Peters, he began the immense task of putting together material that would reflect the modern history of man.

The collection assembled in the Crypt includes 800 microfilmed books that influenced the world, scale drawings of man's inventions, a photographic history of the United States, recordings of great speeches, films of industrial processes, a course in English in case she is no longer spoke, objects of daily life, weapons and scientific instruments, plant seeds, papier mache models of fruit and vegetables, and clothing — in short, a capsule archive of civilization as we knew it in 1940.

The project was completed in May 1940, and the Crypt was sealed for 6,000 years, a time span corresponding to the interval between the first date in recorded history and 1940.

It's rather nice to think that in distant millennia, when we have all been long forgotten, our works will live on intact, to be viewed by generations yet to come with perhaps as much awe as we ourselves bestow on the relics of King Tut. And that Atlanta will still be a center of tourism in 8113 A.D.

NAMESAKES

Atlanta's cities and counties got their names for reasons ranging from the pretty to the practical. Here are some of the stories behind the names, based on Kenneth K. Krakow's *Georgia Place-Names* (Macon: Winship Press, 1975). The years in which cities were incorporated or counties created are in parentheses.

Place-name	Origin
Alpharetta (1858)	Alfarata, the fictional Indian heroine of a 19th century song, *The Blue Juniata.*
Canton (1833)	Canton, China. Named for an attempt by Joseph Donaldson to emulate the Chinese city's famous silk industry by introducing silkworms and mulberry trees to the Georgia town.
Clayton County (1858)	Augustin Smith Clayton (1783-1839), judge and state senator.
Cobb County (1832)	Judge Thomas Willis Cobb (1784-1835), a colonel in the Revolutionary War and later a state congressman.
Conyers (1854)	Dr. Conyers, a banker, who bought the site and right of way for a Georgia Railroad station here.
College Park (1891)	Named in 1895 when Cox College was moved here from LaGrange.

Decatur (1823)	U.S. Navy Commodore Stephen Decatur (1779-1820) of Maryland.
DeKalb County (1822)	Baron Johann DeKalb (1721-1780), who accompanied LaFayette to America and served under Washington in the Revolutionary War.
Douglas County (1870)	U.S. Congressman Stephen A. Douglas (1813-1861), the man backed by the South against Lincoln in the 1860 Presidential campaign.
Fulton County (1853)	Either Robert Fulton (1765-1815), a pioneer of the steamboat, or Hamilton Fulton, a civil engineer who proposed and surveyed the railroad through the county.
Gwinnett County (1818)	Button Gwinnett, a signer of the Declaration of Independence.
Henry County (1821)	Patrick Henry (1736-1799) of Virginia, the man who said, "Give me liberty or give me death!"
Marietta (1834)	Either Marietta, wife of Thomas Cobb, or a joint tribute to two local lovelies named Mary and Etta.
Roswell (1854)	Roswell King, who in 1839 established a cotton mill here.
Sandy Springs	A spring used by Creek Indians and early settlers as a watering hole that bubbles through the sand here near Sandy Springs Circle.

The Economic Pie

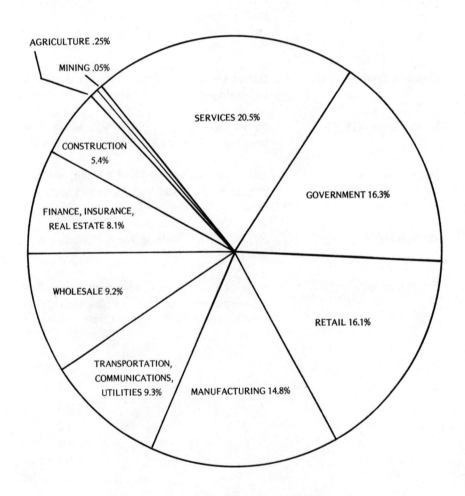

AGRICULTURE .25%

MINING .05%

SERVICES 20.5%

CONSTRUCTION
5.4%

GOVERNMENT 16.3%

FINANCE, INSURANCE,
REAL ESTATE 8.1%

WHOLESALE 9.2%

RETAIL 16.1%

TRANSPORTATION,
COMMUNICATIONS,
UTILITIES 9.3%

MANUFACTURING 14.8%

ATLANTA'S ECONOMY

From the Civil War on, the most outstanding feature of Atlanta's history has been continuing growth, carefully fostered by the city fathers. Through two "Forward Atlanta" campaigns, one in 1925 and one in the 1960s, the Atlanta Chamber of Commerce succeeded in attracting hundreds of new businesses to the city.

Since then, aggressive promotion of the region has continued to draw major industrial and commercial enterprises to the area. Between 1970 and 1980, employment increased from 620,000 to 884,000 — by nearly 43 percent — according to Atlanta Regional Commission estimates.

Atlanta's Base Industries

Atlanta's biggest employer, and the fastest-growing sector in the region, is **services,** including everything from personal to professional services.

Atlanta is sometimes described as a regional service center, meaning that it provides services not just to the metropolitan area but to much of the Southeast. The Atlanta Chamber of Commerce is proud to boast that 439 of the Fortune 500 industrial companies have regional or corporate headquarters in the metropolitan area, from which they serve other parts of the Southeast.

Among the Fortune 500 firms with corporate headquarters in Atlanta are Coca-Cola, Gold Kist, Royal Crown, National Service Industries, and Georgia-Pacific.

In the 1960s, Atlanta added conventions to its economic base by building new hotels downtown, constructing exhibition facilities, and expanding air service to the city. Today, Atlanta is the third largest convention center in the country.

THE INSIDER'S ATLANTA

The second largest share of Atlanta's workforce is in **government** service. This is the effect not only of growth in the region's many local and county governments, and of the fact that Atlanta is the state capital, but also of the increasing federal presence in the city. Indeed, the strength of the downtown office market is partly a result of the high concentration there of federal offices serving the Southeast.

Another important segment of Atlanta's economy is **trade.** Retail trade is the third largest employer in the region, while wholesale trade is also a significant component of commercial activity.

Atlanta is not a heavily industrialized area. Nevertheless, **manufacturing** is the fourth largest employment sector in the seven-county metropolitan area. Companies making transportation equipment are the biggest employers in this category. This is mainly because of the Lockheed-Georgia Company, which makes the giant C-5 and other cargo and military transport planes at its plant in Marietta, and because of the General Motors and Ford auto-assembly plants located respectively in Doraville and Hapeville. Other important manufacturing categories are metals and machinery, food and kindred products, textiles and apparel, printing and publishing, and paper products.

Other rapidly growing sectors of Atlanta's economy are finance, insurance and real estate, and transportation, communications, and utilities. Atlanta is the headquarters of the Sixth Federal Reserve District.

The International City

Atlanta's growing involvement in the international economy is reflected in several ways. Thirteen countries have full-time consulates here, and a number of foreign commercial banks have set up branches in Atlanta in recent years to facilitate international trade.

There has also been a considerable amount of foreign investment in Atlanta, notably from Canada, Europe, and some Arab countries. In addition, a Foreign Trade Zone, designed to promote the assembly here of foreign-made goods, has been established in Shenandoah Industrial Park in Coweta County, just south of the metropolitan area.

Another sign of the growing internationalism of Atlanta is the formation of a World Trade Club by several major local corporations. The club assists companies to develop overseas markets and provides a base of operations and meeting-ground for foreign executives visiting the city. It is headquartered at the Atlanta Merchandise Mart, 240 Peachtree Street, N.E.

The region's exposure to the rest of the world is also assisted by the city-based Southern Center for International Studies, which sponsors visits and luncheon briefings by distinguished foreign visitors and statesmen, as well as educational programs on international affairs.

Downtown

19

The Atlanta Economic Development Corporation

Clearly, Atlanta's employment profile is largely white-collar. The City of Atlanta has adopted an economic development strategy designed to attract blue-collar industries to the city to absorb the city's large pool of unskilled, predominantly Black labor.

The city has also created the Atlanta Economic Development Corporation (AEDC) to lure new employers to the city and retain old ones. The AEDC serves as Atlanta's official contestant in the fierce competition among local jurisdictions in the metropolitan area for new industry.

The Central Business District

Atlanta's central business district has had to face growing competition from surrounding counties. Dispersal of office and manufacturing locations was encouraged by the opening of a perimeter highway (I-285) around the city in 1969. However, the effect on Atlanta's downtown area has been less severe than in many other cities, partly because of the continuing commitment to the area shown by major businesses, and partly because of an ambitious program of downtown construction begun in the 1960s.

Much of this construction was spurred by Atlanta architect-developer, John Portman, whose plans transformed three blocks of downtown Peachtree Street. Portman believed that the downtown area could remain vital if it offered security and open space. He designed his towering Peachtree Center, Hyatt Regency Hotel and Peachtree Plaza Hotel to reflect these amenities, with fountains, waterfalls, and indoor lakes. Portman also developed separate Merchandise and Apparel Marts which offer manufacturers a place to display their wares at trade shows.

The effect of construction by Portman and others was to give the city a glamorous new skyline and much modern office, hotel, and exhibition space. In 1976, the World Congress Center opened. It was developed, like the adjacent Omni International complex, by Portman's main rival, Tom Cousins, and has the largest single-level exhibition space in the nation with further expansion planned.

The rebirth of the Phoenix continues.

Employment By Industry

Industry Group	Employment*
Services	180,848
Government	
Federal	37,031
State	26,757
Local	80,325
Retail Trade	142,547
Manufacturing	130,706
Transportation/Communications/ Utilities	82,154
Wholesale Trade	81,743
Finance/Insurance/Real Estate	71,760
Construction	47,688
Agriculture	2,228
Mining	479
TOTAL	**884,418**

Employment by County

County	Employment*
Fulton	447,297
DeKalb	218,073
Cobb	97,343
Clayton	52,991
Gwinnett	48,671
Rockdale	10,968
Douglas	9,075
TOTAL	**884,418**

*Source: Atlanta Regional Commission, *1980 Employment Data Report.* Data from counties listed above.

21

Coca-
Local Product

Coca-Cola is probably Atlanta's greatest success story. It began in 1886 as a druggist's pain reliever cooked up in a three-legged pot in an Atlanta backyard. Today it "adds life" in 135 countries on every continent. And Atlanta remains the world headquarters of this liquid empire.

Coke did not enrich its inventor, Dr. John S. Pemberton, an Atlanta pharmacist who thought he had developed a cure for headaches. Mixed with carbonated water, however, Dr. Pemberton's syrup "containing the properties of the wonderful Coca plant and the famous Cola nuts" proved, as he advertised, "delicious! refreshing! exhilarating! invigorating!" Still, Dr. Pemberton was happy, two years later, to sell a one-third interest in his product to Asa G. Candler for $500.

Candler, a Georgian who had settled in Atlanta some 15 years previously, later purchased the remaining interest in Coca-Cola and began to vigorously market his new product. Within seven years, he was able to claim that Coca-Cola was drunk "in every state and territory in the United States." And by 1919, when Candler sold his

They Want

City of Atlanta

Atlanta Economic Development Corporation,
1350 North Omni International,
Marietta Street,
Atlanta,
Georgia 30303.
Tel.: 658-7066

Downtown Atlanta

Central Atlanta Progress,
First National Bank Tower,
2 Peachtree Street, N.W.
Atlanta,
Georgia 30303.
Tel.: 658-1877

Cola: Makes Good

interest to Ernest Woodruff, an Atlanta banker, for $25,000,000, Coca-Cola even had a small overseas market.

Woodruff's son, Robert W., who became president of the company in 1923, set himself the task of making Coke a household word throughout the world. This goal has almost been accomplished. In 1978, when China opened its gates to the West, Coke was the first one through.

As befits a legend, mysteries cling to Coke. One mystery is its ingredients. Coca-Cola's biochemists claim that Coke can't be copied, though many have tried. The story goes that only a handful of men in the company know the complete recipe for Coca-Cola. From time to time, rumors fly that the recipe has been discovered in some dusty corner of Atlanta. Company officials smile at these discoveries, but say nothing.

Coke grew so rapidly because Asa Candler and his successors believed devoutly in the power of advertising. So if you're the kind of person who enjoys paying to promote someone else's products, investigate the Coke Retail Store at the Coca-Cola Bottling Plant, 864 Spring Street. It's filled with items flashing the familiar sign.

Your Business

Metropolitan Atlanta

Atlanta Chamber of Commerce,
1300 North Omni International,
Marietta Street,
Atlanta,
Georgia 30303.
Tel.: 521-0845

Georgia

Georgia Department of Industry and Trade,
P. O. Box 1776,
Atlanta,
Georgia 30301.
Tel.: 656-3545

Atlanta's Vital Statistics

County	Population*
Butts	13,665
Cherokee	51,699
Clayton	150,357
Cobb	297,718
DeKalb	483,024
Douglas	54,573
Fayette	29,043
Forsyth	27,958
Fulton	589,904
Gwinnett	166,903
Henry	36,309
Newton	34,489
Paulding	26,110
Rockdale	36,747
Walton	31,211
TOTAL	**2,029,710**
City of Atlanta	425,022

*1980 Census

FOR
YOUR
INFORMATION

Here's a select list of some of the best information sources in Atlanta.

Agency	Information
Atlanta Chamber of Commerce, 1300 North Omni International. Tel.: 521-0845	Newcomer information; labor, market and utilities data.
Atlanta Historical Society, McElreath Hall, 3099 Andrews Drive, N.W. Tel.: 261-1837	Historical.
Atlanta Public Library, 1 Margaret Mitchell Square Tel.: 688-4636	Williams and Georgia Collections: material on Atlanta and Georgia; Ivan Allen Jr. Department of Science, Industry and Government; federal publications, local government documents, plat maps, business and economic data.
Atlanta Regional Commission, 230 Peachtree Street, N.E. Tel.: 656-7715	Estimates of population, housing and employment in the metro area; planning studies of local government services, water resources, transportation, and environmental quality.

Georgia Archives,
330 Capitol Ave., S.E.
  Tel.: 656-2358

County, tax and voter records; land records; county histories, censuses, and genealogical periodicals.

Georgia Department of Industry
  and Trade,
1400 North Omni International,
  Tel.: 656-3545

Local economic development profiles; Georgia Manufacturing Directory; general business references; manpower data; industrial tax information.

Georgia Department of Labor,
Labor Information Systems.
  Tel.: 656-3177

Statistics on employment and unemployment, turnover, hours and earnings in manufacturing; employment projections; data required for affirmative action plans.

Research Atlanta, Inc.
Suite 1105,
134 Peachtree Street, N.E.
  Tel.: 688-5963

Information and data on current issues of public policy in Atlanta.

A more complete listing of Atlanta information sources is available from the Atlanta Chamber of Commerce.

THE POLITICS OF ATLANTA: The Backroom's Overcrowded

The City of Atlanta is administered by a Mayor, who has executive power, and an 18-member City Council with legislative powers. The unincorporated areas of the surrounding counties are run by elected Boards of Commissioners.

The first Black mayor of Atlanta was elected in 1973. He was Maynard Jackson, the son of a distinguished Atlanta family. In 1981 Jackson yielded his title to another prominent Black Atlantan — Andrew Young, former civil rights leader, U.S. Congressman, and Ambassador to the United Nations. Atlanta thus became the first city in the nation to elect into office two successive Black mayors.

Neighbors With Clout

If you're a neighborhood person, you'll love Atlanta. There are approximately 200 officially designated neighborhoods in the city, some with delightful names like Just Us, Cabbagetown, and Druid Hills.

In 1975 these neighborhoods were organized into 24 Neighborhood Planning Units (NPU's). The city's charter requires that its annual Comprehensive Development Plan be drawn up with citizen participation, and the NPU's, through their representatives, are the means by which this occurs.

To find out who represents your NPU and how you can get involved, contact the Bureau of Planning, City of Atlanta (tel.: 658-6306).

Outside the city, many homeowners' associations are active, and participate vigorously in civic debate on issues that affect them.

The multiplicity of city and county government within the metropolitan area, the jealous suspicion each government has of the motives of the others — with the occasional need for temporary alliances among them — all make the manoeuverings of city, county, and state governments in relation to each other a study in intrigue.

In this heady atmosphere of universal one-upmanship, you might think government would be impossible.

But in Atlanta it just adds up to politics as usual.

II

SETTLING IN

West End

HOUSE
HUNTING

Atlanta offers the newcomer a wide range of housing and neighborhoods to choose from. You can select a Victorian mansion in an older neighborhood, or a comfortable contemporary in a brand-new subdivision. You can live close in or far out, in a planned community or one that just grew. You can renovate and revitalize, or you can move in with nothing to do but unpack. You can buy a house for $1 or $1,000,000.

Property (ad valorem) taxes vary not only between counties but between jurisdictions within a county. Generally, however, property taxes in Atlanta are low compared to other parts of the country. Taxes are levied on 40 percent of the assessed value of the property.

You are eligible for a partial exemption from taxation on the first $2,000 of the assessed value of your home if you occupied it on January 1 of the tax year. In all counties except DeKalb, which mails returns, you must personally apply for the "homestead" exemption in the first year you claim it; it is automatically renewed thereafter. Returns must be filed by April 1, except in Gwinnett (February 28) and Fulton (May 1) counties. Take a copy of the warranty deed, or a copy of the sale closing statement. If you live in a city other than the City of Atlanta, you must file a separate return with that city.

The State of Georgia imposes a 3 percent **sales tax** on consumer goods in all counties. In addition, the voters of Fulton and DeKalb counties approved a 1 percent sales tax to pay for the construction of their rapid rail system. Some other counties in the metro area have adopted a 1 percent local option sales tax to meet local revenue needs.

Only two counties in Atlanta, Fulton and DeKalb, have **public transportation**.

How to Find Your Dream Home

Once you've decided where you'd like to live, the next step is to track down the ideal home.

The classified sections of the daily newspapers carry listings of homes for sale. A number of free booklets distributed in supermarkets, banks, and savings and loan associations also carry listings of homes for sale and of new subdivisions under construction.

Chances are you'll rely mainly on a realtor to help you house-hunt. Most of the major real estate companies belong to a computerized multiple listing service covering 12 counties. This service provides real estate agents with a listing of all homes offered for sale by any of the service's 350 member companies. Therefore, the agent you select can probably show you houses offered by companies other than his own.

A number of companies carry listings of vacant apartments in the metro area which you can consult on payment of a fee; you'll find these companies listed in the yellow pages under "apartments." Another useful source is the free directory of Atlanta area apartments, mainly new, that is widely available.

Fixing Up

Once you've found your home, you'll have to keep it up. The Atlanta Public Library's *Toolmobile* can help. The Toolmobile lends electrical hand tools, gardening tools including wheelbarrows and rototillers, and a range of other useful household gadgets to Fulton County residents holding valid library cards. There is no charge, and tools may be kept for up to two weeks. Call the Mobile Service Unit (tel.: 261-5860) for dates and times of the Toolmobile's visits to the library branch nearest you.

REDISCOVERING
THE
INNER CITY

As the symbol of their city resurrected after the Civil War, Atlantans chose the Phoenix. Over the past decade, a group of modern Atlantans has turned to the work of reconstruction, this time giving new life to old houses and aging neighborhoods. The symbols of this new revival are butterflies, rainbows, and rising suns — emblems of hope.

The revival movement began in the decaying grandeur of Ansley Park, spilling over to adjacent neighborhoods as property values in Ansley Park rose beyond reach of a modest budget. The gracious Victorian homes of Inman Park became the next target of the renovators, in turn generating ripple effects in nearby neighborhoods.

In communities all over the city, new life is stirring in old neighborhoods. Drive through Midtown, Virginia-Highland, Candler Park, Grant Park, West End, and you'll see the telltale signs, more graphic than butterflies and suns — the ladder, tools, and paintcans of the home handyman.

In many cases, it was the single action of one man, or of one group, that stopped the cycle of decline.

In *Inman Park,* Robert Griggs bought an ornate and turreted mansion at 866 Euclid Avenue in 1969, and carefully restored it. His pioneering efforts quickly encouraged others to do the same.

In *West End,* a young architect, Wade Burns, bought 25 decayed Victorian homes in a concentrated area of this old (1835), once-prime residential neighborhood, near the West End Mall. He undertook a "gut" rehabilitation of them, replacing nearly everything but their shells. Others soon followed his example. Even the city got in on the act by replacing brick sidewalks and sprucing up the street. Once one of the city's worst slums, the area around the intersection of Oglethorpe and Peeples Streets is now one of its quaintest corners.

Grant Park is still in a state of transition. This residential area grew up around the 100-acre park given to the City of Atlanta by Colonel Lemuel P. Grant in 1883. Today, rocketing housing prices reward the renovators.

If you are considering settling in the Grant Park neighborhood, you can take advantage of the Neighborhood Housing Services (NHS) program. The Grant Park NHS was founded in 1976 by the Federal Home Loan Bank's Urban Reinvestment Task Force, in cooperation with neighborhood residents, the City of Atlanta, and lenders. Its job is to help homeowners who wish to rehabilitate their homes by estimating costs and assisting with financing. For more information, call NHS (tel.: 525-5929).

Atlanta's $1 Houses

No, that's not a misprint. That's a fact. You really can buy a house in Atlanta for $1.

Of course, there's a catch. The house will probably require some work to be made livable; but you have 18 months in which to bring your house up to housing code standards. You must agree to live in it for three years. And to be eligible for the drawing by which houses are allocated you must have good credit and sufficient income to maintain regular payments.

The houses are made available to local governments under the Department of Housing and Urban Development's Urban Homesteading program. For information, contact the City of Atlanta's Department of Community and Human Development (tel.: 658-6764).

Which Neighborhood?

If you're interested in in-town living, you'll want to discover more about the characteristics of different neighborhoods.

One way is to call the City of Atlanta's Bureau of Planning (tel.: 658-6306) and talk to the NPU (Neighborhood Planning Unit) planner responsible for the neighborhood you're interested in. This planner will be able to give you information about the neighborhood and put you in touch with neighborhood residents who can provide an inside perspective.

A nice way of seeing the neighborhood and meeting the people is to join in the annual tour of homes many neighborhoods offer. These tours are generally held in spring or early summer, when local residents open their homes to the public.

ARCHITECTURE
IN ATLANTA

There wasn't much left of Atlanta by the time the Civil War had taken its toll.

Yet traces of that first Atlanta still crop up unexpectedly in odd places around the city. On Fairburn Road, S.W., are the log cabin that was built by pioneer John Cash in 1828 and the decaying Wilson House, with its 20-inch thick slave-built walls, where Sherman once slept.

Dating back to 1850, *Oakland Cemetery*, 248 Oakland Avenue, N.E. preserves architectural styles in family mausoleums. Beneath Oakland's great trees the dead sleep peacefully. Their origins were diverse: prominent and humble, Black and White, Gentile and Jewish, and their graves are marked by the elaborate funerary sculpture that appealed to 19th century tastes.

Short of indigenous antebellum architecture, Atlanta imported some. The *Tullie Smith House* on the grounds of Swan House, 3136 Slaton Drive, N.W., is an example of an 1840 plantation house; it was moved to its present location from DeKalb County. A variety of pre-war buildings have also been assembled and restored in *Stone Mountain Park's Plantation* complex. The oldest of them, Thornton House, is dated 1791; other buildings include an 1826 log cabin, a barn, and a manor house brought from Albany, Georgia.

The antebellum heritage survives more fully in some of the old towns ringing the city.

Nearby *Roswell's* historic square is bordered by homes with the columned facades that are everyone's idea of the South: places like Bulloch Hall (1840), the home of Teddy Roosevelt's mother, Barrington Hall (1842), built by the son of the town's founder, Roswell King, and still in the family, Holly Hill (1842), Mimosa Hall (1847), and The Bricks (1840), an apartment complex built for mill workers and still renting.

Another town that preserves much of its antebellum ambiance is *Madison,* in Morgan County, just outside the metro area. Its buildings were spared by Sherman as a result of the famed eloquence of Senator Ben Hill's pleading. A printed guide to Madison is available from the Madison-Morgan Cultural Center.

Closer to the city, *Covington,* to the east, opens its historic homes to the public every year in spring. A map and description of the buildings on the tour is available from the Newton County Chamber of Commerce. A similar brochure describing notable buildings in the town of *Social Circle* can be obtained from the Walton County Chamber of Commerce.

The Virtues of Victorian

Atlanta came into its own again in the late Victorian age, notably in the *Inman Park* neighborhood. This garden suburb, developed by entrepreneur Joel Hurt in the late 1880's, was Atlanta's first planned community. An electric streetcar line linked Inman Park to Hurt's downtown skyscraper, the eight-story Equitable Building. The car barn that marked the end of the line still stands at 963 Edgewood Avenue, amid the restored dignity of the neighborhood's imposing mansions. Other Victorian enclaves are situated in *Grant Park* and *West End.*

Early 20th century architecture in Atlanta is dominated by the name of Philip Shutze. Shutze is known particularly for the Swan House, Reid House on Peachtree Road, and the dignified elegance of the banking hall in the C&S Bank's downtown headquarters. The gracious style of Hentz, Reid, and Adler, the firm with which he was associated, is stamped on the spacious homes of Druid Hills, Ansley Park, and Buckhead.

Commercial Architecture

Among the most striking examples of commercial architecture in Atlanta are the towering modern structures of the downtown area. These include the Portman buildings, with their lofty atriums and indoor lakes, and the Omni. The new Georgia Power building, on the fringe of the business district, is notable for its teetering, energy-saving facade that slopes outward from ground level.

Soaring Tower Place in Buckhead is a striking example of the use of glass as a building material: it's a disappearing structure whose bulk is barely visible when it takes on the coloration of the Atlanta sky.

But older commercial buildings have their charm too. Perhaps at the head of this category is the Candler Building, 127 Peachtree Street, N.E., with its ornate carvings and round central lobbies on each floor.

Many of the buildings in the old shopping district south of Marietta Street in downtown Atlanta are also of architectural interest. You can obtain a pamphlet describing a walking tour of the district from MARTA (Rider's Digest, May

Bulloch Hall, Roswell

7-21, 1979) or from the Atlanta Historical Society.

In addition, the Atlanta Preservation Center (tel.: 522-4345) conducts walking tours of the historic Fairlie-Poplar district, as well as of Inman Park and Midtown, from April through October.

Mill Communities

When cotton was king, so was the textile industry in Atlanta. A few old industrial buildings survive as reminders.

The mill village of *Cabbagetown*, built on what was then the fringe of Atlanta, has changed little since the Fulton Cotton Spinning Company constructed its first mill there in 1881 in neo-Romanesque style. Two-storied, white-framed housing for the workers was built around the mill between 1886 and 1899, and is still occupied by their successors. The people of Cabbagetown remain an independent community with an identity that has remained distinct from that of the surrounding city. Cabbagetown is located on the northeast corner of the intersection of Boulevard and Memorial Drive.

Less well-known, the *Whittier Mill district,* off Bolton Road, is another cotton-mill village that has survived nearly intact.

The Follies

Atlanta also has a number of buildings that are remarkable less as architecture than as examples of fantasies made real. One such building is the Fox Theatre which was saved from demolition by a massive community effort. The "Save the Fox" signs you'll see everywhere, are distributed not by opponents of bloodsports, but by persons anxious to restore the Fox to its former Moorish grandeur, complete with elaborate interior decor, tented roof and star-spangled skies.

Another example of the fantastic school of architecture is the mausoleum of Westview Cemetery. Its design is said to be an example of the Spanish Baroque style, and it is so strikingly out of place in the heart of Dixie that it is worth a visit. The mausoleum is said to be the largest structure of its kind under one roof, with room for 11,444 entombments.

For Further Reading

– – – –	*The American Institute of Architects Guide to Atlanta* (Atlanta: AIA Atlanta Chapter, 1975)
– – – –	*Atlanta Historic Resources Workbook* (Atlanta: Urban Design Commission, 1978)
Elizabeth M. Sawyer & Jane Foster Matthews	*The Old in New Atlanta* (Atlanta: JEMS Publications, 1978)

Architects may also be interested to know that a specialized bookstore serves their needs. It's the Architectural Book Center in the Cain Tower of Peachtree Center, 229 Peachtree Street, N.W.

RATE
YOURSELF

Nobody enjoys getting a utility bill. But did you know that you can influence your own bill — not just by conserving energy, but by using mechanisms provided by State government? One of these mechanisms is the Georgia Public Service Commission (PSC); another is the Georgia Consumers' Utility Counsel.

The PSC was created by the Georgia General Assembly to regulate the rates and quality of service of privately-owned utilities. In Atlanta, that means Georgia Power, Atlanta Gas Light and Southern Bell. If you're served by a municipally-owned company or electric membership corporation, the PSC can't help you.

How the PSC Works

The PSC regulates the rates a utility may charge, determines how costs are borne by different classes of users, and investigates consumer enquiries about utility bills.

When a utility wishes to increase the rates it charges its customers, it must file an application for permission to do so with the PSC. By law, the PSC must permit the utility to earn a "reasonable" rate of return on equity. But it also has the power to determine what constitutes a reasonable return, usually by calling in expert testimony. In addition, the PSC regulates how rate increases should be allocated between different classes of users, residential and industrial. By law, these determinations are always made after the public has had a chance to be heard.

How You Can Use the PSC

*You elect the five commissioners who head the PSC. These commissioners serve for staggered six-year terms, and are responsible for setting utility rates and determining PSC policy.

*You have the right to speak at public hearings when any rate application is made. The PSC requires utilities to advertise publicly the date on which hearings are to be held. If you'd like to testify, you need only appear at the PSC hearing room at 244 Washington Street on the day appointed and sign up to speak. Normally, hearings are held when a rate increase is applied for, but a hearing can also be held on petition of an individual or group, or at the instigation of the PSC.

*If you have a question about your utility bill, you can call the PSC's special hot line (tel. 656-4562) and your case will be investigated. Your first recourse should always be to the utility concerned, but if you are not satisfied, the PSC's trained consumer relations group can help you.

The Georgia Consumers' Utility Counsel

This office was created by the state legislature specifically to represent residential customers and small businessmen at utility rate hearings before the PSC. The Counsel represents these users as a class, and not as individuals.

The Counsel's staff includes lawyers, accountants, researchers and consumer relations personnel. His job is to analyze all the elements in the costs a utility wishes to pass on to consumers. If he concludes that the consumers he represents should not legitimately have to pay for these costs, he will argue the case against the utility's application before the PSC.

If you have a problem with your bill (gas, electric, or telephone), you can discuss it with the Counsel's consumer expert (te.: 656-3982). Complaints are not individually dealt with, but if they are sufficiently common, the Counsel may take them up with the PSC on behalf of all residential and small business users.

Nitty Gritties

Atlanta's utilities are supplied by a multiplicity of sources. The accompanying table should help you locate the company serving your city or county.

Georgia Power's *Residential Customer Handbook* and Atlanta Gas Light Company's *Serving You With Natural Gas* explain how to start, stop, and save on electricity and gas. Atlanta Gas Light also sells and repairs gas appliances, and its staff of home economists (tel.: 572-0190) offers gas-saving hints, speakers, and audio-visual aids for educators (tel.: 572-0768).

Garbage is collected either by municipalities or by private contractors, depending on the city or county concerned. The City of Atlanta supplies each house with a free "Herbie the Curbie" — a tough-looking garbage can on wheels. Backyard pickup is also available for a fee; it is provided free for the disabled and those over 70 years old.

Service	Supplier	Deposit	Telephone
Electricity	Georgia Power Co.	Yes	325-4001
Gas	Atlanta Gas Light Co.	Yes	522-1150
Telephone	Southern Bell	Sometimes	529-8611

41

WATER SERVICES

City/County	Notice Required	Notice In per.	Phone	Deposit	Billing	Telephone
Atlanta/ Fulton	24 hrs.	X	X	0	Monthly	(Street names beg.) 658-6521 A-E 658-6522 F-M 658-6523 N-Z 572-2276 Roswell/ Alpharetta
Clayton	24 hrs.	X	—	Yes	Monthly	961-2130
Cobb	24 hrs. 7 days	X	X	Yes	Monthly	422-0222
DeKalb	24 hrs.	X	X	0	2-monthly	371-2641
Gwinnett	24 hrs.	X	X	Yes	Monthly (deposit included in 1st bill)	962-1513

GARBAGE COLLECTION

City/County	Collection Automatic	Private	Landfill	Billing	Telephone
Atlanta	X	—	—	In property taxes	351-0215
Clayton	—	X	X	Quarterly	478-9911 ext. 344
Cobb	—	X	X	Varies	429-8900
DeKalb	X (call to arrange)	—	X	Quarterly	294-2100
Fulton: Dalrymple Rd. — Atlanta city limit	X	—	X	Quarterly	572-2271
Dalrymple Rd. — Chattahoochee	optional		X	Quarterly	572-2271
N. of Chattahoochee	—	X	X	Varies	572-2271
South Fulton	—	X	—	Varies	572-2271
Gwinnett	—	X	X	Quarterly	962-1400

III

GETTING AROUND

MARTA Station, Decatur

WHAT'S
IN A
NAME?

When it came to christening the streets of Atlanta, imagination failed. A few Names Suitable For Streets seem to have been selected by committee and then applied, with tireless repetition, to any situation that offered. That's one of the pitfalls of getting around Atlanta.

Of course, the trained ear rapidly learns to make subtle distinctions. The Peach and the Pine adorn lanes, ways, circles, drives, avenues, courts, roads and streets, often in company with a Lake. The insider skillfully seizes on the qualifier (lane, way, circle, etc.) and hangs on to it for dear life if he wishes to reach his destination. A hint: the road is often the main thoroughfare, off which the avenues, courts, etc. lead.

But there are some things you just have to know: for example, that West Peachtree Street is counterbalanced by and dead-ends into Peachtree Street (there is no East). Beyond the downtown area, Peachtree Street metamorphoses into Peachtree Road. As you head north, specify your destination: is it Peachtree Road, North Peachtree Road, New Peachtree Road (there are two Olds), or perhaps even Peachtree Industrial Boulevard?

Be alert to distinguish Ashford-Dunwoody, Chamblee-Dunwoody and Peachtree-Dunwoody Roads. Note that East Paces Ferry flows into West Paces Ferry Road, but West Paces Ferry and Paces Ferry run parallel beyond their intersection. Remember that there are two Roswell Roads (neither to be confused with Lower Roswell Road) each a busy thoroughfare; the only thing they have in common is that they both lead, from different starting points (Marietta and Atlanta) to the City of Roswell.

Got it?

45

A Plethora Of Peachtrees

You know that everything's peaches in Georgia. This is, after all, the Peach State.

But the peachtree is not native to Atlanta. And nobody is quite certain why it is so strongly identified with the city. It was so even before the advent of the White man: Standing Peachtree was the name of a large Creek Indian village situated on the banks of the Chattahoochee.

There are two possible explanations. One is that the village was named after a single peachtree standing atop a nearby hill. The second is that a lone pine tree oozing resin, or pitch, inspired the village's name.

Whatever the true origin, there was no escape from Peachtree This and Peachtree That once the name was applied to Fort Peachtree. This fort was constructed on the site of the Indian settlement between 1812 and 1814. A reconstruction of Fort Peachtree can be visited at 2630 Ridgewood Road, N. W. It is open from 8 am - 4 pm weekdays.

RELAX—
AND ENJOY THE RIDE

That's the slogan of MARTA, the Metropolitan Atlanta Rapid Transit Authority. It's true too. MARTA's buses and trains are safe, clean, comfortable — and convenient.

MARTA buses cover some 30 million miles a year, and carry riders to the furthest reaches of DeKalb and Fulton Counties. The rapid rail system, when completed, will be a 53-mile long system of underground, aerial and surface railroad, stretching from Doraville in the north to Hartsfield Airport in the south, and from Hightower Road in the west to Avondale in the east, with a spur line branching off to Proctor Creek and a public housing complex. So far, only the east-west line and a short segment of the north-south line have been completed.

The opening of the first rapid rail segment, from Avondale station to the Georgia State station, in June 1979 was a cause for much celebration. Crowds turned out to watch the first train roll in, and its driver found himself an instant celebrity whose autograph became a coveted commodity. The west line, from Hightower Station to Five Points, opened in December 1979 and, within a month, MARTA planners were watching, almost with disbelief, their most optimistic ridership projections far exceeded.

The Making of MARTA

Jubilation was mixed with relief. For, from the start, there were sceptics who doubted whether MARTA could make good its claims. The system was intended to do so many things: to provide a means of mass transportation that would make mobility easier, reduce dependence on the automobile, and cut

47

Meeting Up With MARTA

MARTA schedule information is available by calling 522-4711 or by writing to MARTA Community Relations, 2200 Peachtree Summit Building, 401 West Peachtree Street, Atlanta, Georgia 30308. MARTA also publishes a map of the entire transit system; you can obtain one free by writing to MARTA or calling at MARTA's Ride Store at 62A Peachtree Street, opposite Central City Park.

Fares include a transfer from one bus to another, or from bus to train, on a one-way, continuous journey. You'll need exact change. Alternatively, you can purchase MARTA's monthly Transcard which permits you to make as many journeys and stops as you wish.

Buses

MARTA operates five Park and Ride Lots where patrons may leave their cars and catch express buses downtown. These lots are located on Abernathy Road at Georgia 400, Buford Highway at Oakcliff Road in Doraville, Memorial Drive at Kensington Road, Hammond Drive at Perimeter Mall, and Fourth Street at East Mountain Drive in Stone Mountain.

MARTA also operates an L-Bus or Lift Bus Service for the handicapped. For more information, call 586-5440. Easy accessibility for the handicapped has been built into the rapid rail system.

Trains

The rapid rail system operates Monday through Friday from 5:30 am to midnight, 6:25 am to 11:49 pm Saturdays and Sundays. Trains run at 12 to 15 minute intervals, and every 10 minutes during rush hours. There are parking lots at MARTA stations, but some are usually full, so ride to the station with a friend if possible.

traffic congestion; to bring new shoppers and businesses into the downtown area and other business districts located at transit "nodes", and to provide a showcase for the city's architectural and artistic talents.

The sceptics questioned MARTA's ridership projections, its ability to revitalize old business districts, and the value of expenditures on art.

It took three tries (in 1965, 1968, and 1971) before voters in Fulton and DeKalb agreed to build and pay for the system. Gwinnett and Clayton are, however, also represented on the MARTA Board because their citizens had earlier accepted the idea in principle.

Laying the Track

In 1975, after four years of planning, construction of the first phase of the rail system began. The transit network that eventually results will be a marriage of technology and art.

Its technological achievements include construction of a mile-long subway tunnel beneath the central business district, using techniques more appropriate to deep-sea and deep-space exploration, to protect workers from the risk of "the bends" as they emerged from the high-pressure world below the surface to the low-pressure one above.

Another engineering feat was the construction of the Civic Center station over the busy I-85 interstate highway — without diversion of traffic. The station consists of a 140-foot wide bridge carrying two railway tracks and two platforms over six lanes of traffic, and ultimately over 12. Atop its roof runs the rerouted West Peachtree Street. The entire structure is supported only in the middle and at the ends. From the highway, the station has the appearance of a passing train.

Other MARTA stations display a cheerful profusion of aesthetic styles, including colorful murals, the starkly curving sculptures of the King Memorial Station, ceramics, and glass mosaics. Art comes in stripes, triangles, and organic forms, and in rainbow hues.

Impressive and efficient. Can one ask more?

THE
OUTSTRIPPED
AIRSTRIP

Atlantans are inordinately proud of their airport — William B. Hartsfield Atlanta International Airport, to be exact. It won't be long before you learn that it's the second busiest in the world, handling over 18 million passenger departures and more than 550,000 aircraft landings and take-offs a year. From Atlanta, there is frequent air service to over 145 cities in America and several in Europe.

Why does a regional capital have such a busy airport? Because two major airlines, Delta (which is based in Atlanta) and Eastern, use Hartsfield as a "hub" scheduling most of their flights in such a way that travelers from other cities must pass through Atlanta to reach their ultimate destinations. As a result, only 28 percent of all passengers boarding planes in Atlanta begin their journeys here; the rest merely transfer from one plane to another.

In 1978 direct international service from Atlanta to Europe and Great Britain was inaugurated. The number of European and South American cities served from Atlanta is expected to grow steadily, and already includes London, Brussels, Frankfort, Amsterdam, and Mexico City.

Biggest and Best, So They Say

In September 1980 Atlanta's new air terminal was opened for use, amid much hoopla.

Hartsfield may, grudgingly, yield place to Chicago's O'Hare in terms of the number of passengers processed, but it yields to none in size and quality of the new terminal.

Built at a cost of nearly $500 million, the complex's dimensions are staggering. The distance from the main passenger terminal to the most distant concourse is 1.1 miles. The passenger terminal and concourses cover 50.5 acres. There are 12,000 parking spaces.

Nothing of the latest in electronic gadgetry has been omitted. There are moving sidewalks, computer-guided electric trains that whisk passengers back and forth, telephones with amplifying devices to serve the deaf, and an automated pre-pay parking system.

The airport also houses $450,000 worth of art by contemporary artists, some well-known, others not. The work of the 14 artists represented ranges from neon sculptures to canvases, tapestries and photographs.

The ingenious design of the new terminal raised the number of airplane loading positions from 72 to 140, and passenger-handling capacity from 39 million to 52 million. A new air cargo complex was also constructed to handle the growing volume of air freight passing through Atlanta.

Yet already it is forecast that the expanded airport will be saturated before the decade is out. But there will be no more expansion at Hartsfield — there is simply no more room. Either Atlanta must build a second airport (a plan which exists on paper) or it must learn to live within its limits.

You can reach Hartsfield by car or taxicab. In addition, Northside Airport Express (tel.: 455-1600) operates buses to the airport from Marietta, Dunwoody, Tucker, and Memorial Drive locations. MARTA's No. 72 bus provides service from the corner of Auburn Avenue and Park Place downtown at half-hour intervals.

The Little Guys

In addition to Hartsfield Airport, there are a number of smaller airports in the Atlanta region that accommodate general aviation, or light aircraft. The biggest of these are Fulton County's Brown Field and DeKalb County's Peachtree-DeKalb Airport. Other general aviation airports in the seven-county region are McCollum (Cobb County), Stone Mountain (DeKalb County), South Expressway (Clayton County) and Gwinnett County Airport. You can find out about other general aviation airports in the metropolitan area by contacting the Georgia Department of Transportation, Bureau of Aeronautics (tel. 393-7353). There is also a military airport, Dobbins Air Force Base, in Cobb County.

51

RAILROADS

In 1937, 102 passenger trains arrived in Atlanta each day, and 500 merchandise and packing cars departed over 15 lines. So reported proudly the commemorative volume, *The Atlanta Centennial 1837-1937.*

Today, only one passenger train a day pulls into Brookwood Station, but Atlanta's importance as a freight-train junction has grown.

The Southern Crescent is the sole survivor of Atlanta's grand old passenger trains, and it has survived the Congressional axe only by a narrow squeak.

The Crescent links New York and New Orleans. It departs New York daily on an overnight journey which takes passengers through Newark, Trenton, Philadelphia, Wilmington, Baltimore, Washington D.C., and Greenville before the Crescent steams into Atlanta. Hence, the Crescent chugs on through Birmingham, Meridian, and points south to reach New Orleans. For reservations, call Amtrak (1-800-874-2800).

Freight Trains

Freight trains have fared much better than their passenger-carrying counterparts. Some 150 freight trains pass through Atlanta daily. In total, these trains draw approximately 11,000 railcars through Atlanta every day, railroad officials estimate. They provide a vital link in the region's economy, connecting Atlanta to the Northeast, the Midwest, and the rest of the Southeast.

The Family Lines System operates just over half of these trains; the remainder belong to Southern Railway. The Family Lines System includes Seaboard Coast Line, as well as the Louisville and Nashville, Atlanta and West Point, and Georgia Railroads. The system provides service to Miami, Richmond, New Orleans, Louisville and Chicago. Its main marshalling yard is Tilford Yard in Marietta.

Southern Railway, which also operates the Central of Georgia Railroad, marshalls its trains through the huge Inman Yard, and serves Washington D.C., Birmingham, New Orleans, Jacksonville, and Cincinnati.

Museum Pieces

If you wish that airplanes had never been invented, and that the world still traveled in soothing lurches on metal rails, you'll be glad to know that iron horses which have passed their prime have a pasture of their own in Atlanta.

Tended by the Atlanta Chapter of the National Railway Historical Society, the Southeastern Railway Museum displays vintage models on a 12-acre site between Norcross and Duluth. The exhibit includes steam locomotives, cars from the Nancy Hanks and other passenger trains of the 1940's and 50's, a reconstruction of the 100-foot Central of Georgia turntable, and even a privately-owned Georgia Power streetcar that once prowled the streets of Atlanta.

The Museum is located on Buford Highway, north of I-285, at Berkeley Lake Road. Open Saturdays 9 am - 5 pm. Tel.: 476-2013.

Flying Machines

Veterans of foreign wars and domestic service, and victims of the age of technology, a group of aging aircraft awaits a final resting place in Atlanta.

Assembled by members of the Georgia Historical Aviation Museum (tel.: 449-0703), the group includes a 1920's N3N made by the Naval Aircraft Factory, a Mitchell bomber of the type that destroyed Japanese cities in World War II, a DeHavilland L20 and a Fairchild PT 19. The Museum also possesses an extensive collection of aviation memorabilia.

Horseless Carriages

Among the 40 or so vintage vehicles corraled in Stone Mountain Park's auto museum are some that were old when Model T's were young. Oldest of these is an 1895 Fugier made in Paris. All of the cars are originals, lovingly restored to their pristine gloss, and several are one of a kind — among them the car used by the celebrated Mr. Buck Rogers in his movies.

Open daily, 10 am - 6 pm. Admission fee.

IV

LEARNING
EXPERIENCES

Apollo 6 Module, Fernbank Science Center

ATLANTA'S PUBLIC SCHOOLS

Next to choosing a career and a spouse, selecting a school for your child is probably one of the most careful decisions you will ever face.

This section provides some information to aid parents in making this decision.

Some Basics

Your child can enter kindergarten in any public school system in Georgia if he has turned five on or before September 1 of the year in question. In some school systems, he can get started even earlier. For example, the Atlanta School District offers federally-funded pre-school education to children whose families meet certain criteria.

In order to enroll your child in a public elementary school in Georgia he must have turned six on or before September 1 of the year in which he is to be registered. He must also have been inoculated against a battery of childhood diseases: diptheria, pertussis, tetanus, polio, measles, mumps and rubella.

Atlanta's Public School Systems

There are 10 school districts within the Atlanta metropolitan area. They are those of the cities of Atlanta, Buford, Decatur, and Marietta and of Clayton, Cobb, DeKalb, Douglas, Fulton and Gwinnett counties.

As a general rule, these school districts are operated independently of local governments. Policies are set by elected school boards.

THE INSIDER'S ATLANTA

Choosing a Public School

The Georgia Department of Education does not evaluate or rank the metropolitan area's school districts in terms of educational quality. However, the Department's Statistical Services Division makes available certain data that can be used to compare systems. Some of this information relates to enrollments, number of students graduating, teacher-pupil ratios, average per pupil expenditures, average teacher salaries, number of library books per student, and other measures.

Data on a school system as a whole can be misleading, however. Educational quality may vary from school to school within a single system. Educators suggest that parents take the following factors into account in making this decision:

*Check test scores   The State tests reading and math abilities of all students in public schools in Grades 4, 8, and 10. Ask to see the scores recorded at the school you are interested in, and compare them with scores at other schools in the area. School principals and school districts can show you these results; they can also be obtained from the Georgia Department of Education's Student Assessment Office. Educators warn, however, that parents should not rely solely on these scores, since the average recorded at a good school in an area with a varied population may be lower than the quality of instruction merits.

You can also ask to see results of "norm-referenced" achievement tests administered independently by school districts. Based on samples, tests such as the Iowa and California tests of basic skills, compare achievement levels in individual school districts with national scores.

*Talk to the principal and inspect the school
*Talk to parents of children attending the school
*Tour the neighborhood
*Learn what additional educational facilities the school or school system offers, including art, music, career education, and sports facilities. In a few school systems, parents are required to pay for elective courses.

Larger school systems, such as those of Atlanta, Fulton, and DeKalb, tend to have more resources at their disposal. Among them are planetaria, enriched learning opportunities for gifted children, alternative academic environments like DeKalb's two Open Campus high schools and Atlanta's Downtown Learning Center for students who are bored or drop out of conventional classes.

The Atlanta school system offers six magnet schools emphasizing particular areas of expertise. These special programs are open to all students in the system who meet the entrance qualifications. Oldest of the magnet schools is the Northside School of Performing Arts in Northside High School. Others are the North Fulton Center for International Studies, the Grady High School School of Communications, the Benjamin E. Mays Center for Science and Mathematics, the Roosevelt High School Center for Information Processing and Decision-Making, and the Harper High School Center for Financial Services.

Among the most remarkable facilities in the area is the DeKalb school system's Fernbank Science Center. The Center offers some 300 courses in various scientific disciplines that are used by many school systems, but only DeKalb students can pursue independent study courses at the Center.

EDUCATIONAL INFORMATION SOURCES

Public School Systems

System	Phone
Atlanta, City of 224 Central Ave., S.W. Atlanta, Ga. 30335	659-3381
Buford, City of 181 Bona Rd., Buford, Ga. 30518	945-2713
Clayton County 120 Smith St., Jonesboro, Ga. 30236	478-9991
Cobb County 47 Waddell St., Marietta, Ga. 30060	422-9171
Decatur, City of 320 N. McDonough St., Decatur, Ga. 30030	373-5344
DeKalb County 3770 N. Decatur Rd., Decatur, Ga. 30032	296-2000
Douglas County P. O. Box 1077 Douglasville, Ga. 30133	942-5411

Fulton County	768-3600
786 Cleveland Ave., S. W.	
Atlanta, Ga. 30315	
Gwinnett County	963-8651
52 Gwinnett Dr.,	
Lawrenceville, Ga. 30245	
Marietta, City of	422-3500
P. O. Box 1265	
Marietta, Ga. 30061	

Parent and Community Groups

Apple Corps*	522-4662
250 Georgia Ave., S. E.	
Atlanta, Ga. 30312	
Council of Intown Neighborhoods	876-5451
& Schools,	
949 Plymouth Road, N. E.	
Atlanta, Ga. 30306	
Northside Atlanta Parents	
for Public Schools,	
P. O. Box 52563	
Atlanta, Ga. 30355	

Private Schools

Atlanta Area Association	
of Independent Schools	237-9286
c/o Trinity School	
3003 Howell Mill Rd., N. W.	
Atlanta, Ga. 30327	
Georgia Association	
of Independent Schools	436-5425
3209 Isoline Way	
Smyrna, Ga. 30080	

*Apple Corps is a non-profit educational information service serving the Atlanta public schools, and promoting greater community involvement in the school system.

Catholic Schools,
   Atlanta Archdiocese   881-6643
756 W. Peachtree St., N.W.
Atlanta, Ga. 30308

Bureau of Jewish Education   873-1248
1745 Peachtree Rd., N.E.
Atlanta, Ga. 30309

Accrediting Agencies

Georgia Accrediting   912-685-6345 (am)
   Commission,
605 South Kennedy St.,
Metter, Ga. 30439

Southern Association of   897-6100
   Colleges & Schools,
795 Peachtree St., N. E.
Atlanta, Ga. 30365

Schools for the Handicapped

The Help Book,
United Way,   522-0110
100 Edgewood Ave., N.E.
Atlanta, Ga. 30301

Pre-School Education

*The Preschoolers' Resource
Book: A Guide for Atlanta Area
Parents,* by Gail V. Goodwin.

    This is an excellent starting point, concisely detailing facilities and phil-
osophies at preschool establishments in Fulton and DeKalb counties. It also lists
teachers of arts and crafts and other classes geared to toddlers. Available in
Atlanta and DeKalb public libraries.

ATLANTA'S PRIVATE SCHOOLS

There are scores of private schools in Atlanta. They offer preparation for any type of future you may desire for your child, whether it be the independent life of a rugged individualist or the carefully-circumscribed path to success awaiting graduates of the Ivy League.

Of course, such freedom of choice is expensive. It costs from $1,000 to $3,000 a year in tuition alone to keep a child in a private school, the exact amount depending on the grade-level and school attended. So it behoves the parent to look carefully.

What Should Parents Look For?

We asked officials of the Georgia Association of Independent Schools what features to look for in a private school. Here are their suggestions:

*Is the school accredited? The two universally-respected accrediting agencies in Georgia are the Southern Association of Schools and Colleges (SACS) and the Georgia Accrediting Commission (GAC).

Accredited schools must submit annual reports to the accrediting agency and are re-evaluated every five years. Non-accreditation does not necessarily mean that a school is inadequate, but it does place the burden of investigating its quality and standards on the parent.

Pre-school or kindergarten programs are generally not accredited, unless they are part of an accredited elementary school. However, SACS has prepared an experimental set of kindergarten standards which you can use as a guide in choosing a school for your toddler.

*What is the condition of the school's physical plant? What facilities are available to students? These facilities may range from adequate to extraordinary. For example, Westminster, one of Atlanta's most exclusive "prep" schools, offers, in addition to better than average academic and sports facilities, stables for 50 horses, riding rings and rifle ranges. Another, the Woodward Academy, boasts a $1-million fine arts center with classrooms and theater.

*What is the financial condition of the school?

*What is the school's religious orientation? Many of the private schools in Atlanta are affiliated with a religious denomination, including a variety of Protestant creeds, the Catholic Church and the Jewish faith. Some schools are nondenominational and others are secular.

*What are the qualifications of the teachers?

*What is the attitude and spirit of the school?

As in the case of the public schools, it is important for parents to visit the schools they are interested in and to talk with the principal and teachers. And, say the experts, you would be well advised to begin this process at least a year before you plan to send your child to school. In the case of schools of particular prestige, parents have been known to enter their child's application for admission at birth!

Town And Gown

Atlanta's universities offer a number of services to businesses. In addition, a number of faculty perform private consulting work.

Agency	Service	Telephone
Georgia Institute of Technology		
Engineering Experiment Station	Technical assistance; Economic development assistance; Testing and measurements; Energy & environmental studies; Specialized services.	894-3411
Georgia State University		
Economic Forecasting Project	Quarterly analyses of economic trends.	658-3282
Small Business Development Center	Seminars; Technical information & assistance; Free consultations.	658-3550
Center for Professional Education	Management seminars.	658-2745
Contract Research Division	Data on incomes and employment; Research for governmental agencies.	658-4250

IVORY
TOWERS

Some people measure a region's degree of civilization by its distance from Boston. This is an idea which has always been particularly infuriating to the South, which is pretty far from Boston.

Atlanta, though it boasts no Harvard, can perhaps be described as a minor-league Boston, or as the Boston of the Southeast. For it possesses, in addition to four Ph.D.-granting institutions, eight colleges and universities granting lower degrees, four community colleges, eight theological institutions, three non-accredited law schools, and a technical institute.

While Atlanta's four largest universities possess certain elements in common, each has its own sense of unique mission, of a particular constituency to be served. Two of these universities, Georgia Institute of Technology and Georgia State University are state-supported and two, Emory and Atlanta University, are private.

The Atlanta University Complex

The AU complex is one of the most remarkable institutions in Atlanta. It is the oldest center for higher education in the city, and it is composed of a cluster of Black colleges that have produced or been associated with some of the nation's most outstanding men and women, including Dr. Martin Luther King, Jr. and W. E. B. DuBois.

The colleges in the complex — Clark, Morris Brown, Spelman, Morehouse, and the seven schools comprising the Interdenominational Theological Center — operate independently but cooperatively. Atlanta University provides the graduate education for them all. Chartered in 1867, it is also the oldest institution in the complex.

Morehouse College for men moved to its present site in 1888; it was founded in 1867 in Augusta, Georgia as the Augusta Institute. Its female counterpart is Spelman College, named after the mother of Mrs. John D. Rockefeller; Spelman's buildings were completed around 1890.

The two coed colleges in the AU complex are Clark (founded 1868) and Morris Brown, which achieved college status in 1894 and began life in 1881 as a high school founded by the African Methodist Episcopal Church.

The newest addition to the AU colleges is the Morehouse Medical School which began operating in 1978.

Apart from its academic importance, the AU complex is also significant architecturally. A number of its buildings are on the National Register of Historic Sites, and as a whole, the complex is considered one of the most aesthetically valuable in Atlanta.

Emory University

Founded in 1836 in the little town of Oxford, Georgia, Emory moved to Atlanta in 1915. It's especially strong in the fields of law, theology and medicine.

And in its ability to raise funds. In 1979, Emory received a gift of $101-million for its endowment from Robert W. Woodruff, former chairman of the Coca-Cola Company. The gift is believed to be the largest single donation ever made to a university, and it brought the total of Woodruff's philanthropic contributions — most in the form of gifts from "an anonymous donor" — to an estimated $350-million.

Georgia Institute of Technology

Nationally, Tech is perhaps the best known of Atlanta's educational institutions. Tech opened its doors in 1888 with two buildings on a four-acre campus, and now sprawls over 295 acres with more than 120 buildings.

Tech is known for its engineering school. The Institute is a pioneer in research into alternative energy sources especially solar studies. It is also a leader in electronics and environmental research, including the development of weather radar.

The Institute's many facilities include a 5 megawatt nuclear reactor used to study the effects of radiation, to analyze atomic structure, to make radioisotopes, and for other peaceful purposes; a solar furnace and solar thermal test facility; facilities for the study of electronic warfare; and a pyrolysis system that converts waste materials into useful fuels.

Georgia State University

GSU is an urban university, and it sees its main task as being to serve the

In the Quad, Agnes Scott College

needs and help solve the problems of urban communities. It was founded in 1913 as Georgia Tech's Evening School of Commerce. In 1969, after many vicissitudes, GSU entered its present incarnation as a full-fledged university.

One of the great advantages GSU offers students is the ability to earn a degree either full-time or part-time, since courses are also offered at night. In addition to the normal range of academic offerings, among which its M.B.A. program is particularly highly regarded, GSU also has a College of Allied Health Sciences, a College of Urban Life offering M.S. degrees in criminal justice, human resources and urban studies, and programs in commercial music and recording and in hotel administration.

Among the smaller institutions of higher learning in Atlanta are Oglethorpe and Mercer Universities, Agnes Scott College, Southern Technical Institute, the Atlanta College of Art, and Kennesaw College, now a four-year school. The region is also rich in two-year schools like Atlanta Junior College, Clayton Junior College, and DeKalb Community College.

These Chimps Aren't Chumps

The biggest collection of great apes in the world is in Atlanta. And that's no reflection on the city's population.

The collection includes chimps, orang-utans and gorillas as well as some 1,500 other non-human primates, and it belongs to the Yerkes Regional Primate Research Center attached to Emory University.

From the apes, scientists hope to learn something about man, including the effects of weightlessness in space, drugs, and other conditions on primate physiology. So they study the animals' nervous systems, and how they behave, socialize and communicate.

The Center is named after its founder, Dr. Robert M. Yerkes, who started the collection with two chimpanzees. Today, the Center has two facilities, one at Emory, the second at a field station near Lawrenceville where a select group of chimps and orang-utans live in style on private islands in a man-made lake.

Probably the Center's most famous member is Lana, a chimp who can "talk." compose music, distinguish colors, and tell "more" and "less." Lana has been taught to communicate with her keepers by means of a computer-based vocabulary and a word-alphabet composed of geometric symbols. By pressing several symbols, she can form sentences. The Lana experiment has been so successful that the technique has been adapted for use by retarded children who cannot talk.

Two other Yerkes chimps, Austin and Sherman, have also learnt to converse. Each has a vocabulary of 56 symbols, and they have been taught to communicate with each other by means of these symbols, asking for food and tools. Researchers have found that the chimps understand each other much better when they talk in symbols than when they rely on gestures and grunts.

Darwin would be delighted.

GROWING OLDER
AND WISER

If it's worth teaching, somebody's probably teaching it in Atlanta. You can learn anything from how to frost a cake, renovate a house, or surf the white water to how to die rich, if not famous. Best of all, these courses are surprisingly inexpensive.

The institutions listed below offer instruction to the general public; in addition, many clubs and religious organizations offer courses to their own members. Arts and crafts classes are listed in Part V.

Institution/Program	Courses	Location	Phone
Atlanta Area Technical School/Off-Campus	Home Economics Business Education	1560 Stewart Ave., SW 419 Northside Dr., NW	758-9451 233-5483
DeKalb Community College/ Informal Enrichment Program	Varied	DeKalb County High Schools.	296-4400
Emory University/ Evening at Emory	Varied	1380 S.Oxford Rd., NE	329-6000
Emory University/ Senior University	Varied — academically oriented for senior citizens	849 Houston Mill Rd.	329-6000
Georgia State University/ Season for Self	Varied	University Plaza	658-3456
Oglethorpe University/ Non-Credit Courses	Varied	4484 Peachtree Rd., NE	233-6662

V

CULTURAL
AFFAIRS

Jugglers, Atlanta Arts Festival

THE
ARTS
IN ATLANTA

Culturally, Atlanta is a mixed bag. It may never give birth to any radical new artistic venture that could shake the world, but a spirit of innovation and experimentation is sweeping through a growing core of serious artists migrating to the city.

Over the past decade, there has been an explosion in the visual as well as the performing arts in the city. A multitude of new artistic ventures, spontaneous, imaginative, and often struggling, have injected fresh vitality into Atlanta's cultural life. Professional and amateur theatre, poetry reviews, new art galleries, crafts, experimental dance, non-commercial cinema and honky-tonks are busting out all over.

The cornerstone of traditional culture in Atlanta is the *Memorial Arts Center*, 1280 Peachtree Road, N.E. This large complex was built as a tribute to the memories of 106 Atlantans, many of them leaders of the city's arts community, who perished in a plane crash at Orly, France in 1962 while on a tour of European museums. The complex includes a symphony hall, two theaters, an art museum and a school of art.

But all over the city, abandoned school buildings are entering new incarnations as cultural centers.

Of these, one of the most intriguing is that founded by *Nexus Inc.* at 360 Fortune Street, N.E. This arts center began in 1977 when an organization of photographic artists called Nexus leased the dilapidated and vandalized building from the Atlanta School Board. Soon, other organizations had joined in to share in the renovation work and obtain inexpensive space to pursue their art. In addition to Nexus, the complex now houses a fine arts press, art galleries, dance and drama companies, and a metal foundry to cast large sculptures. And here professional artists starting out on their careers, whose work has been judged of

73

sufficient merit, can rent inexpensive studio space.

The *Neighborhood Arts Center,* 252 Georgia Avenue, S.W., is another abandoned school building that has been renovated and turned into a cultural beehive. The Center serves as a base for a number of musical, literary and theatrical groups and houses an art gallery, but its prime purpose is instructional. Classes are offered in art, dance, music, and writing techniques.

The signs of the burgeoning of the arts in Atlanta are clearest in the neighborhoods closest to the city's heart. Downtown you can see them in the large murals that are part of the *Urban Walls* project sponsored by the downtown business organization, Central Atlanta Progress, and in the new MARTA stations that were designed to be showcases of the city's art. City government has even adopted a policy of applying one percent of the cost of construction of any municipal building to the purchase of visual art to adorn it.

The Medicis of Atlanta: City Government

One of the most active forces in Atlanta's arts community is the City of Atlanta's Department of Cultural Affairs. Acting on the premise that art is not only good for the soul but good for the municipal economy, the Department funds and supports a variety of artistic activities. The bucks the Department spends produce three bangs: they support local artists, encourage the growth of related businesses and employment, and provide the public with fantastic freebies.

You can while away a summer evening on the lawns of Piedmont Park while the Atlanta Symphony plays for your pleasure, or catch a noontime concert at the amphitheater in Central City Park downtown — both free. Equally easy on the pocketbook are the three-day Dance Festival of Atlanta held in June, and the Third World Film Festival in October. Piedmont Park comes alive again in fall with the Free Jazz Festival in September and the downhome Festival of Georgia Folklife, both sponsored by city government. There are also special programs to bring art and music to the city's housing projects and poorer neighborhoods.

Other public support for the arts in Atlanta comes from the Georgia Council for the Arts and the National Endowment for the Arts.

Folk Arts

A collection of more than 700 pieces of authentic Georgia folk art and folk implements exists in Atlanta. Painstakingly collected by Dr. John Burrison, who teaches English at Georgia State University, the items in the collection cover a period ranging from 1800 to the present. The collection is temporarily in storage until a home can be built for it at the Atlanta Historical Society's headquarters.

Though time was when the ancient crafts were confined to the rural fastnesses of the South and the inaccessible hills of Appalachia, many have now come down to the plains. A useful directory of Georgia craftsmen has been compiled by the Georgia Council for the Arts and Humanities (tel.: 656-3863), 1627 Peachtree Street, Atlanta, Ga. 30309.

The big event in the craftsman's year is the *Atlanta Arts Festival* held in Piedmont Park each year in May. Artists and craftsmen from all over the country are attracted to it, and it's a fine place to have a child's face finger-painted or to purchase a piece, watch a play or catch a free concert. Scores of smaller craft shows take place all over the metropolitan area from spring through fall.

Here's a list of some of the best places in Atlanta to learn traditional crafts and many others. In addition, the parks and recreation departments of most other counties and cities in the Atlanta area offer occasional courses. Contact the one in your area to find out what's available.

Sponsor	Center	Address	Telephone
City of Atlanta	Chastain Arts & Crafts Center	135 West Wieuca Rd., N.W.	252-2927
	Southeast Neighborhood Center	215 Lakewood Way, S.E.	627-4474
DeKalb County	Callanwolde Arts Center	980 Briarcliff Rd., N.E.	872-5338
	Arts in South DeKalb	80 South DeKalb	241-2453
	DeKalb North Arts Center	5345 Roberts Drive Dunwoody	394-3447
Fulton County	Abernathy Park Arts & Crafts Center	294 Johnson Ferry Rd.	252-1799
— —	Neighborhood Arts Center	252 Georgia Ave., S.W.	523-6458

HIGH
ART

It's name suggests a lofty aestheticism, a sort of Olympian remoteness from the ordinary affairs of men. Yet the title is an accident of fate. The High Museum of Art earned its name for no better reason than that it stands on property bequeathed to the arts by the widow of Joseph Madison High.

The ivory tower image the name conjures up is misleading; community outreach is one of the Museum's most important goals. Its programs for children have earned national recognition.

To assess the true worth of the High's holdings, one must wait until a planned, $15 million new museum is constructed and in use on an adjacent site in 1983.

Outstanding among these holdings, according to Eric Zafran, curator of European art, is the fine Haverty collection of 19th century American land-scape paintings. This collection contains works by a wide range of artists, in-cluding George Inness, Thomas Moran, and Martin Johnson Heade, and works by the early 20th century group known as "The Eight."

The museum also has a distinguished photography collection, some excel-lent 19th and 20th century prints, and a tasteful collection of decorative arts, as well as a notable group of early 15th and 16th century paintings, the gift of the Kress family.

You can find out about current exhibits and programs by calling the High's hotline, tel.: 892-4444.

Gifts play a very important role in the High Museum's fortunes. For the gallery is remarkable in having no budget for acquisition of art works. The col-lections, therefore, rely solely on the generosity of well-wishers and on grants from the National Endowment for the Arts.

The museum staff hopes that the new building, with its 150,000 square

76

feet of exhibition space (more than three times more than its present quarters) will encourage potential donors, permit larger and more important traveling exhibitions to be shown, and make it possible to arrange loans from other museums of works in areas not represented at the High.

The recent appointment of three curators — for European art, contemporary art, and the decorative arts — is also expected to have a positive effect. The curators' duties will include reviewing existing holdings and arranging exhibitions in their areas of expertise. In addition, one of their most important tasks will be to stimulate the growth of private collections in Atlanta by advising art patrons in the selection of works. This will help the High in two ways. It will "raise the tone" of art awareness in the city, and it will enable the museum to draw on these private collections for special exhibitions.

Amid all this hopeful ferment, the High could well adopt "Excelsior!" as its motto. Higher — and Higher!

Galleries Galore

Atlanta is still young, and so is its artistic tradition. It's a sign of the city's gradual maturing that the number of galleries showing work by internationally, nationally, regionally, and locally-known artists is growing steadily.

Here's a list of some of the best places to view fine art. Check hours of opening before you visit.

Gallery	Works Shown	Telephone
A Touch of Glass, 1850 Lawrenceville Hwy. Decatur.	Fine American crafts; graphics, paintings.	329-1486
Alexander Gallery 442 E. Paces Ferry Rd.	Naive, folk art.	266-2311/ 266-2792
American Art Gallery 56 E. Andrews Dr., N.W.	Fine crafts.	231-0535
Ann Jacob Gallery, Peachtree Center 230 Peachtree St., N.E.	Sculpture by international artists; fine art.	659-7084
Atlanta Artists' Club 2979 Grandview Ave., N.E.	Works by members.	237-2324
Atlanta Gallery of Photography 3077 E. Shadowlawn Ave., N.E.	20th Century fine art photographers.	233-1462
Art in Atlanta/ Ten to Four 511 E. Paces Ferry Rd.	Contemporary and transitional graphics by American and European artists.	237-1960

CULTURAL AFFAIRS

Artists Associates Gallery 3261 Roswell Rd., N.E.	Members' works.	261-4960
Chastain Arts and Crafts Center Gallery 135 W. Wieuca Rd., N.W.	Contemporary Southern art and crafts.	252-2927
Crystal Britton Gallery 15 Baltimore Pl., N.W.	Contemporary and traditional African and American art; vintage photographs.	892-8835
Charlie's Gallery 3025 Peachtree Rd., N.E.	Original graphics, sculpture, pottery, etc.	231-0550
Eva Mannes Gallery 288 E. Paces Ferry Rd.	Sculpture, paintings, monoprints and watercolors.	237-8477
Fay Gold Gallery 3221 Cains Hill Pl., N.W.	Art and photography by established contemporary artists.	233-3843
Frances Aronson Gallery 56 E. Andrews Dr., N.W.	18th-20th century European and American paintings.	262-7331
Gallerie Jude 2126 N. Decatur Rd.	Paintings and photography by Atlanta artists.	634-6568
Garnett Street Gallery 158 Garnett St., S.W.	Crafts and fine art by local and southeastern artists.	688-2292
Goethe Institute 400 Colony Square	Modern German artists.	892-2388
Heath Gallery 416 E. Paces Ferry Rd.	20th Century American artists.	262-6407
Image South 1931 Peachtree St., N.E.	Contemporary regional artists.	351-3179
Kipnis: Works of Art 277 E. Paces Ferry Rd.	American contemporary art, sculpture, drawing, paintings.	233-3958
Kraskin/Mitchell Gallery 414 E. Paces Ferry Rd.	Original graphics by leading international artists.	261-8198
Nassau Visions Gallery 1176 ½ W. Peachtree St., N.E.	Works by Atlanta artists.	872-0262
Nexus Gallery 360 Fortune St., N.E.	Photography; contemporary fine arts.	577-3579/ 688-1970
Odyssey Studio of Fine Art 546 E. Paces Ferry Rd.	Contemporary etchings and graphics; sculpture, pottery.	261-3060
Olympia Galleries 267 E. Paces Ferry Rd.	19th Century photographs; 18th-20th century paintings, drawings, prints.	237-5660
Phoenix Arts and Theatre Co. 992 Gordon St., S.W.	Work by Black artists.	755-5511

Photographic Investments Gallery 730 Miami Circle, N.E.	19th Century photographic images.	233-3012
Romare Bearden Gallery Neighborhood Arts Center 252 Georgia Ave., S.W.	Contemporary paintings, sculpture, paintings.	523-6458
Signature Shop 3267 Roswell Rd., N.E.	Crafts.	237-4426
Stanley and Schenck Peachtree Center 231 Peachtree St., N.E.	Regional and local artists and sculptors.	525-4728
Women's Art Collective 114 10th St., N.E.	Work by women artists.	872-8045

MUSIC,
PLAY!

Classical music in Atlanta thrives mainly under the umbrella of the Atlanta Symphony Orchestra (ASO), but a number of smaller ensembles are beginning to cast their own shadows and attract their own followings.

The ASO was founded in 1944. During the past decade, under the directorship of Robert Shaw, it has earned a national reputation enhanced by the acclaim of critics in New York and Washington, D.C.

For the formal fall and winter season, the ASO combines a judicious mixture of classical and contemporary music in its repertoire. Its particular strength is choral work, exemplified by the traditional highlight of the symphonic year: the annual performance of Handel's *Messiah* on the eve of Christmas.

But the season's not all solemn. In its new "Winter Pops" concert series at the Fox Theatre, the Orchestra joins with jazzmen to shake out the shivers.

In summer, the Symphony's mood is light, and few things are more delightful than the weekly Sunday-evening gatherings on the lawns of Piedmont Park, where the lazy sounds of summer combine with favorite melodies played by a famed orchestra to pleasure the senses and relax the mind. It's all free, too! If you like your music more robust, there are the annual "Pops" Concerts in Chastain Park, where great jazz artists join forces with the Orchestra to make the crowds swing. And low-priced Saturday morning "Coffee Concerts" at Symphony Hall will help you introduce your youngsters to the rich world of the classics.

Chamber Music

Until quite recently, chamber music in Atlanta was largely restricted to friendly soirees at home. And there is still a need, according to Juan Ramirez, founder of the Atlanta Virtuosi, to establish chamber music as part of the cultural life of the city. Ramirez hopes to do it through performances and by introducing youngsters to chamber music at an early age.

Although chamber music still has some way to go before it achieves the popularity of the symphony or the ballet, there is a growing interest in the genre among the Atlanta public. Four professional ensembles have been formed in the city in the past five years to serve this expanding audience. All perform works ranging from the Baroque to the contemporary.

In addition, several Atlanta colleges and universities present concerts and recitals by well-known visiting ensembles as well as by faculty members and students. Recitals are also sponsored by the Atlanta Music Club (tel.: 233-2131) and in a Virtuoso Pianist series under the auspices of the Memorial Arts Center (tel.: 892-2414).

The city possesses a core of serious composers of new music as well. A number have grouped themselves into an organization called The Music Alliance (P.O. Box 5462, Atlanta, Ga. 30307). Through its performing group, the Atlanta New Music Ensemble, the Alliance enables Atlanta composers to have their work performed in public, along with other works by 20th century composers. The Alliance also maintains an experimental jazz group, the Jazz Bones Orchestra, which plays original works and produces concerts with nationally known artists.

Opera

The annual visit of the New York Metropolitan Opera has been a highlight of the Atlanta social calendar since 1910. For a week each May, the Civic Center teems with opera buffs tastefully toiletted, togged, and tuxedoed for the occasion.

The most recent incarnation of indigenous professional opera here is The Atlanta Civic Opera Association. The Civic Opera is dedicated to producing both the popular traditional as well as creative contemporary operas, and to combining world renowned singers with regional talent.

Two smaller companies provide showcases for local singers. The Phoenix Opera puts on three productions a year, while the Shoestring Opera Company — so named because of its budget — attempts to provide an opportunity for talented individuals from all sections of the musical and theatrical community to gain experience in a professional production.

Gilbert and Sullivan add the finishing touch to Atlanta's musical makeup. A new company, Southeastern Savoyards, presents the partners' works in the best D'Oyly Carte tradition.

Summer Symphony, Piedmont Park

A
MUSICIAN'S
ATLANTA

Ensemble	Auditorium	Telephone
Atlanta Symphony Orchestra	Symphony Hall Memorial Arts Center 1280 Peachtree St., N.E.	892-2414
Chamber Music		
Atlanta Chamber Orchestra (40 pc.)	Recital Hall Georgia State University Arts and Music Building.	873-9080
Atlanta Chamber Players (8 pc.)	Varied.	872-3360
Atlanta Virtuosi (12 pc.)	Academy of Medicine 875 W. Peachtree St., N.E.	378-0864/ 934-0141
Lanier Trio	Varied	634-5292
Contemporary Music		
Music Alliance	Varied	223-5343

Opera

Atlanta Civic Opera Association	Fox Theatre 660 Peachtree St., N.E.	872-1706
New York Metropolitan Opera	Atlanta Civic Center 395 Piedmont Ave., N.E.	262-2161
Phoenix Opera Company	Cobb County Civic Center 548 Clay St., Marietta	255-1128
	Peachtree Playhouse 1150 Peachtree St., N.E.	
Shoestring Opera Company	Emory University Theatre Alumni Memorial Building Emory University	351-5134
Southeastern Savoyards		396-0620

University Faculty/Guest Artist Recitals

Agnes Scott College	Presser Hall East College Ave., Decatur	373-2571 ext. 230
Emory University	Glenn Memorial Auditorium N. Decatur Rd., N.E.	329-6666
Georgia State University	Recital Hall Arts & Music Bldg., cnr. Ivy/Gilmer Sts.	658-2349

The Virtuoso

There's no need to be a virtuoso to play in a symphony orchestra. Several community orchestras in the Atlanta area enable the talented amateur to enjoy the thrill of performance and the pleasure of joining others in making music without the dedication a professional career entails.

There is even a guild of change ringers who practice "the ancient and glorious art of change ringing bells."

Here is how to find out more.

Ensemble	Contact	Telephone
Atlanta Chamber Opera Society	Robert Bloom	378-0064
ASO Chorus	Atlanta Symphony	892-3600 Ext. 211
Collegium Musicum	Emory University, Dept. of Music	329-6445
DeKalb Choral Guild	William Baker	469-3773/ 457-7553
DeKalb Music Theatre	Jim Bradford DeKalb Community College, Music Department	272-1520
Marietta Chorale	Jeannette Sheeler	422-1892
North Atlanta Community Chorus	Gene Mikell	971-1777
The Marching Abominables (a marching band for "anyone who thinks he can play.")	Larry Woodring	378-3346

Amateur

St. Anne's Guild of Change Ringers	Mark Phillips	231-4588/ 525-0406
	Derek Wilsden	941-7312

Sing Along

A number of choral groups give songsters the chance to put their voices to beautiful use. Most groups require an audition, and some choral experience and the ability to read music are preferred.

Ensemble	For more information contact	Telephone
Atlanta Community Orchestra	Prof. J. N. Demos, Georgia State University	658-2349 394-3256
Atlanta-Emory Orchestra	Emory University, Department of Music	329-6445
Cobb Community Orchestra	Betty Bennett	973-6540
DeKalb Community Orchestra	Thomas Anderson Department of Music, DeKalb Community College	292-1520
DeKalb Wind Ensemble	DeKalb Community College	292-1520
DeKalb Jazz Ensemble	Alan Beach Department of Music DeKalb Community College	292-1520
Emory Consort (early music)	Emory University, Department of Music	329-6445
Emory Wind Ensemble	Emory University Department of Music	329-6445

SHALL
WE
DANCE

One of the less well-known facts about Atlanta is that it is home to the first American ballet company founded outside New York City. That company, which began in 1929 as the Dorothy Alexander Dance Art Group, is still on its toes after 50 years, but under a new name, the Atlanta Ballet.

Designated the State Ballet Company of Georgia by Governor Jimmy Carter in 1973, the Atlanta Ballet tours extensively both in Georgia and throughout the nation. Its repertoire includes classics of both traditional and modern ballet as well as original works created by choreographer Tom Pazik. The traditional highlight of the Ballet's annual season is its Christmas performance of The Nutcracker at the Fox Theatre.

Atlanta also has many smaller dance companies. Though they perform throughout the year, the high point is reached in July, when the city-sponsored Atlanta Dance Festival gives them a well-publicized opportunity to show their paces. Most of these companies perform original work, often choreographed by their individual directors, and operate in conjunction with a school. Many tour widely.

Company	Dance Genre	Telephone
Atlanta Ballet 1404 Spring St., N.W.	Ballet	873-5811
Carl Ratcliff Dance Theatre Atlanta School of Ballet, 3215 Cain's Hill Pl., N.E.	Modern	266-0010

City Center Dance Theatre 1843 Cheshire Bridge Rd., N.E.	Ballet/Jazz/ Modern	873-4888
Company Kaye 1060 St. Charles Ave., N.E.	Modern Dance/ Mime	876-6998
Dance Unit 360 Fortune St., N.E.	Avant-garde/ group-developed choreography	261-4861
Ruth Mitchell Dance Studio 3509 Northside Parkway, N.W.	Classical ballet in a contemporary manner	237-8829

VI

GOOD TIMES

At the Pub

IN
THE HEAT
OF THE NIGHT

Night in Atlanta brings out the raunchy and the refined. . . and all persuasions in between. The devotees of jazz, theatre, and the symphony head their separate ways. The swinging singles choose their hunting grounds. The barflies swarm. And the shadows come alive.

In Buckhead, around the intersection of Peachtree, Roswell, and West Paces Ferry Roads and adjacent streets, a profusion of bars, restaurants, and music halls appeals to many tastes.

In southwest Atlanta, a strip along Campbellton Road is a hot spot for cool cats. Casual elegance is the rule for patrons of this cluster of discos, bars, and jazz clubs.

Virginia-Highland — the neighborhood around the intersection of Virginia and North Highland Avenues — is earning a reputation for inventive cuisine.

And, in sundry locations throughout the city, buxom ladies bare their bosoms.

There's something for everyone.

A Note

This book contains few lists. That's because so many establishments are here today, gone tomorrow. Besides, newspapers publish up-to-date listings every week. Here, where names are named, it's because the establishments have a certain degree of fame — or at least notoriety — not to be exhaustive, or indicate quality.

Belly Up To The Bar, Boys!   And Girls

Perfume and powder before you head for any of Atlanta's many singles

93

bars. In these arenas, predators of both sexes prowl. Or would, if seats and space weren't at a premium.

A singles bar is easily distinguished from a bar of the ordinary variety by the big central counter which occupies much of its space, by the jostling and certifiable overcrowding of bodies around this central counter, and by the lean and hungry look in the eyes of its patrons. Some notable names in this category: élan in Park Place, Harrison's on Peachtree, T.G.I. Friday's in The Prado on Roswell Road.

If you're not single or desperate, you may seek company and entertainment in other environments. Every community has its favorite neighborhood bars, where friends gather for beer and conversation.

In the Little Five Points area, the Little Five Points Pub is the preferred watering hole; while in Virginia-Highland Manuel's, George's, and Moe's and Joe's are institutions, and Taco Mac's offering of 122 beers from all over the world is justly famed.

In Midtown, the Stein Club on Peachtree Street has survived - even thrived on — the many vicissitudes of the neighborhood and continues to attract a following of original thinkers. And in Buckhead, Aunt Charley's and the Churchill Arms draw their own crowds of regulars.

Do You Wanna Dance?

"It's a tempotheque," says one. "It's a sensorium instead of a disco," says another. "It's nightlife in the fast lanes," says a third. The subject? Atlanta's discotheques.

Limelight in Buckhead is sometimes described as all three. Prepare for a long wait here among an assortment of oddly-dressed and underdressed citizens. Cisco's and Mr. V's Figure 8 on Campbellton Road are famed; and the San Souci's rotation of sets of live and recorded music has been popular with Atlantans since 1969. Other discos are listed in the Yellow Pages.

Well, it don't mean a thing if it ain't got that swing! The golden days of the big bands live on at Colony Square. Every Friday, from 5 to 8 p.m., those who yearn for that gilded age gather here and Tea Dance to Teegarten and other great names of the swing era. At the Lark and Dove in Sandy Springs, Sunday night brings out a big band live; and at Johnny's Hideaway near Buckhead any night's a good night for recorded 1940's music.

There's nostalgia on tap, too, at Stagger Lee's in College Park and at Studebaker's and Yesterday's in Buckhead. In these establishments, twisting and shouting and other hallmarks of the 1950's and 60's are still in. South Carolina beach music floats across Ocean Beach South on Roswell Road.

Tingles, in Dunfey's Hotel near I-75, offers a medley of disco and ballroom dancing, as does Earl's in Broadview Plaza; and several of the clubs listed under the "Live, In Concert" section have dance floors too.

Dinner Is Served!

Until fairly recently, the chains dominated the restaurant scene in Atlanta. They still tend to do so in the surrounding counties. But within the city itself, the number of owner-operated eateries offering personal attention to detail is growing, as is the number of ethnic restaurants of all types.

You won't find a restaurant listing in this book, partly for the reasons already given, and partly because we lack the courage of *Brown's Guide to Georgia's* restaurant reviewer. This intrepid individual roams far and wide reviewing and grading restaurants. Every month readers' letters pelt him with brickbats and bouquets. And every month, bloody but unbowed, he rises again to review some more. We have watched his performance with awe and admiration; but we are not brave enough to copy it. Readers are referred to this periodical for restaurant ratings. Another useful publication, annually updated, is *Cuisine Atlanta* (Atlanta: Cuisine Publications, Inc.) which publishes restaurant menus.

Some eateries deserve mention, however, because they are institutions. Among them are The Varsity, a hot-dog stand that basks in Georgia Tech's custom and claims to be the world's largest drive-in restaurant, Nikolai's Roof at the Hilton where reservations are recommended to be made months in advance, and Paschal's, the favorite hangout of Atlanta's black politicians during the 60's, where plans were hatched and strategies plotted.

Bon appetit!

LIVE,
IN CONCERT!

For the price of a drink and, occasionally, a cover charge, you can hear live music in Atlanta any night of the week. Jazz. Or rock. Or country. Or what you will.

While nightclubs and bars often feature local groups, Atlanta is on the touring circuit for the biggest names on the national and international scene. Superstars shine at The Omni downtown or at the Fox.

Jazz has its ardent devotees here. The Atlanta Jazz Forum (tel.: 758-2422) publishes a monthly newsletter and holds regular meetings for jazz enthusiasts, and a group called The Jazz Disciples keeps tabs on local jazz history. For amateurs, there's a jam session Monday nights at the Lark and Dove. In addition, the Music Alliance (tel.: 223-5343) provides a base for an experimental group called the Jazz Bones Orchestra.

Here's a list of some of the best places to catch a live concert; *Creative Loafing's* weekly Vibes Calendar is a useful guide to what's playing. Check the individual club for hours of opening; most don't close until the wee hours.

Club	Open	Telephone
	Country and Western	
The Buckboard 2080 Cobb Parkway S.E. Smyrna	M-Sat.	955-7340
Country Greens 5231-B Memorial Dr. Stone Mountain	F-Sun. (live) Open 7 days	294-7417

96

Country Roads 6400 Hillandale Rd. Lithonia	W-Sat.	482-9131/ 482-9555
Mama's Country Showcase 3952 Covington Highway Decatur	W-Sat.	284-6262
Mark Anthony's S. Central Ave. Hapeville	W-Sat. (live) Open M-Sat.	768-3764
Nashville Sound 3611 N. Cobb Parkway Acworth	F, Sat.	974-2503
Scooters Music & Dance Hall 6521 Roswell Rd., N.E.	7 days	255-7295
Silver Saddle 3889 Covington Highway Decatur	M-Sat.	289-5796

Rock 'n Roll

688 688 Spring St., N.E.	Tu-Sat.	874-7500
The Bistro 1102 W. Peachtree St., N.E.	W-Sat.	872-5324
Clarence Foster's 1915 Peachtree Rd., N.E.	Tu.-Sat.	351-0002
Hedgens 3236 Roswell Rd., N.E.	7 days	233-1216
The Rock Showcase 951 Clay St. Marietta	M-Sat.	429-9509

Jazz/Rhythm and Blues

200 South 2004 Campbellton Rd., S.W.	M-Sat.	755-3232
Chaps 5830 Roswell Rd., N.E.	7 days	252-0587
Dante's New Place 3380 Peachtree Rd., N.E.	7 days	266-1500
e.j's 128 E. Andrews Dr., N.E.	W-Sun. (live) Open 7 days	262-1377
Ivey's South 587 Virginia Ave., N.E.	7 days	897-1044
The Lark and Dove 5788 Roswell Rd., N.E.	Tu.-Sat. Open 7 days	256-2922
Paschal's 830 M.L. King Jr. Dr.	M-Sat.	577-3150
Rumors 2112 N. Decatur Rd.	Tu.-Sat.	636-8600
Scandels 3850 Roswell Rd., N.E.	M-Sat.	261-8200
Walter Mitty's Jazz 818 N. Highland Ave., N.E.	7 days	876-7115

Varied

Carlos McGee's 3035 Peachtree Rd., N.E.	7 days	231-7979
& 3360 Chamblee-Tucker Rd.	7 days	451-5850
Good Ol' Days 3013 Peachtree Rd., N.E.	7 days	266-2597
& 5841 Roswell Rd., N.E.	7 days	257-9183

Washtub Band, Festival of Georgia Folklife

Harvest Moon Saloon 2423 Piedmont Rd.	7 days	233-7826
Little Five Points Pub 1174 Euclid Ave.	W, F, Sat., Sun. (live) Open 7 days	577-7767
Moonshadow Saloon 1880 Johnson Rd., N.E.	7 days	881-6666

Top Forties

Charley Magruder's I-285 at Powers Ferry Landing	7 days	955-1157
The Great Buckhead Saloon 3330 Piedmont Rd., N.E.	7 days	231-2326

Cabaret

Club Atlantis 265 Peachtree St., N.E. (Hyatt Regency)	Tu.-Sun.	577-1234
The Plush Room 683 Peachtree St., N.E. (Hotel York)	Tu.-Sun.	874-9200

Comedy

The Punch Line 280 Hilderbrand Rd., N.E.	Tu.-Sun.	252-5233

ALL
THE WORLD'S
A STAGE

"Don't put your daughter on the stage, Mrs. Worthington," Noel Coward begged. But, in spite of that, the lure of the spotlights has created a growing pool of theatrical talent in Atlanta, and new acting companies continually spring up to absorb it.

The theatres they perform in range from the luxury of the Alliance Theatre in the Memorial Arts Center to the bare-bones functionality of small, shoestring operations. While New York has its Broadway and off-Broadway plays, Atlanta can almost be said to have its Peachtree and off-Peachtree productions. The more established theatres — the Academy, the Alliance, the Fox, and the Peachtree Playhouse — are located on Peachtree Street, while many of the newer, more experimental companies are concentrated in or near the Little Five Points area near Inman Park.

The great plays of the master playwrights are seen here less often than some might wish, but there's no shortage of original material.

One of the most vivid signs of this is the annual *New Play Project* held for two weeks in June. The Project was launched in 1978 by the Academy and Alliance Theatres. It attracts new works submitted by playwrights from the Southeast. Those plays selected are staged by companies chosen from the 11 that participate in the Project, and performances are often followed by informal discussions. A number of plays first seen as part of the project have later been incorporated successfully into the performing company's regular season.

In Atlanta theatre, even the deaf are provided for. An organization called Stage Hands Inc. has interpreters "shadow" actors in special performances, signing and miming the spoken words so that the deaf can "hear."

Winter is the dramatic season for most local companies, but summer offers its own diversions. That's when an organization called Theatre of the Stars brings Broadway musicals to the city, usually with celebrities in leading roles.

Company	Theatre	Emphasis	Telephone
Academy	Academy Theatre 1137 Peachtree St., N.E.	Classical/Modern	892-0880
Alliance	Alliance Theatre Memorial Arts Center 1280 Peachtree St., N.E.	Classical/Modern	892-2414
Alliance	Studio Theatre Memorial Arts Center 1280 Peachtree St., N.E.	Experimental	892-2414
Just Us	Peachtree Playhouse 1150 Peachtree St., N.E.	Varied	252-8960
Onstage Atlanta	420 Courtland Ave., N.E.	Modern classics	897-1802
People's Survival Theatre		Black experience	799-1597
Seven Stages	430 Moreland Ave., N.E.	Original/ avant-garde	523-7647
Southern Theatre Conspiracy		Innovative/ comedy	688-1970
Theatre of the Stars	Civic Center 395 Piedmont Rd., N.E.	Broadway hits (summer)	523-1879/ 252-8960
Theatre of the Stars	Peachtree Playhouse 1150 Peachtree St., N.E.	Drama/ Comedy (winter)	252-8960
The Theatrical Outfit	Performing Arena, 1025 St. Charles Ave., N.E.	Original material, experimental/also performances for institutional groups	872-0665
Upstairs at Gene & Gabe's	1578 Piedmont Ave., N.E.	Musical revue	892-2261

SCREENS

If films with million-dollar budgets bore you, and The Force was not with you after "Star Wars", and the jaws in "Jaws" gaped no wider than your yawn, there's good news for you in Atlanta. Intermixed with liberal showings of blockbusters and a goodly sprinkling of porn, non-commercial and foreign films find their way to a few select cinemas.

Atlanta draws film-makers from much of the Southeast because of the inexpensive editing facilities made available at IMAGE, a non-profit resource center for independent, non-commercial film-makers. In addition to its regular twice-weekly screenings of such films, IMAGE, in conjunction with the High Museum of Art, sponsors the annual Atlanta Independent Film and Video Festival where the work of independent film-makers is judged by nationally known figures.

Another highlight of the cinematic year in Atlanta is the annual Third World Film Festival held at the Rockefeller Fine Arts Center of Spelman College in the Atlanta University Complex. Held in October, the festival — it's free — is sponsored by the city's Department of Cultural Affairs.

Here is a directory of cinemas showing foreign films, oldies but goodies, and independents.

Theatre	Film Fare	Telephone
Atlanta Public Library and branches 1 Margaret Mitchell Square	Varied/ documentary (free)	688-4636
The Bijou Ansley Mall 1544 Piedmont Ave., N.E.	Foreign	892-7520

Goethe Institute 400 Colony Square cnr. 14th & Peachtree Sts.	German films, English subtitles (free)	892-2388
Hill Auditorium High Museum of Art, Atlanta Memorial Arts Center, 1280 Peachtree St., N.E.	American classics/ independents/ films on artists (free)	892-3600
IMAGE 972 Peachtree St., N.E. Suite 213	Independents	874-4756
Lefont Tara 2345 Cheshire Bridge Rd., N.E.	First run/foreign	634-6288
Rhodes 1500 Peachtree St., N.E.	Repertory Foreign	876-7919
The Screening Room Broadview Plaza 2581 Piedmont Rd., N.E.	First run/foreign	231-1924
The Silver Screen Peachtree Battle Shopping Center 2369 Peachtree Rd., N.E.	Older/ "off-the-wall"	237-5505

VII

PRINT
&
PRATTLE:
The Media in Atlanta

Henry Grady Statue, Marietta Street

READ
ALL ABOUT IT!

There are seven daily newspapers in metro Atlanta, umpteen weeklies including a business newspaper, a glossy monthly, and a business magazine.

The *Atlanta Constitution,* the city's oldest newspaper, was founded in 1868; its afternoon counterpart, *The Atlanta Journal,* in 1883. Each has contributed one famous writer to the nation's literature: the *Constitution,* Joel Chandler Harris, author of the Uncle Remus tales, and the *Journal,* Margaret Mitchell, author of *Gone With The Wind.*

The *Constitution* has also produced two famous editors. Henry Grady's fervent advocacy of a New South promoted the industrialization of the region; and Ralph McGill's support of racial compromise, in the era of desegregation of the 1950's and 1960's, did much to enable the city to accept change peacefully, and to avert the bloodshed and violence that marked the period in neighboring states. Of this period, McGill wrote, in his book *The South and the Southerner:*[1]

> There is almost an ecstasy which is quite indescribable, in
> seeing, and feeling, a city slowly but surely reach a decision
> and act on it. For a time, one lives a shared experience which
> is deeply rewarding.

Both the *Journal* and *Constitution* are owned by the Cox corporation. On Saturdays and Sundays, and on public holidays, they merge to become *The Atlanta Journal-Constitution.*

The metropolitan area's other dailies, the *Gwinnett Daily News, Marietta*

[1] Boston: Little, Brown and Company, 1964.

Daily Journal, News-Daily of Clayton County, and *Rockdale Citizen,* cover local news; the *Atlanta Daily World* serves the Black community as do the weeklies, *Atlanta Inquirer* and *Atlanta Voice.* Local news and social events are also highlighted in the 25 weekly "neighborhood" newspapers published by Marietta-based Neighbor Newspaper, Inc.

The weekly *Atlanta Business Chronicle* publishes news of interest to the entrepreneurial community. This constituency is served, as well, by *Business Atlanta,* a slick monthly magazine put out by Communication Channels, Inc., an Atlanta-based publisher of numerous trade magazines as well as the glossy monthly *Atlanta.*

Of Atlanta's once-abundant supply of "alternative" newspapers, only one is left: *Creative Loafing* is useful for its weekly entertainment listings — and it's free.

Good reading!

The *Atlanta Daily World*

On August 5, 1978 the *Atlanta Daily World* celebrated its golden jubilee. It was a 50th anniversary marked by tributes from many quarters to a newspaper that proudly claims to be the first successful Black-owned and controlled daily in the U.S. — and one of only two still around.

The *World* was started in 1928 by William Alexander Scott II and his brother, C. A. Scott. Its purpose, in the words of C. A. Scott, was "to give constructive and inspiring news to our Negro peoples, create jobs and prove that our race could produce an important business," with "the idea of removing racial barriers and eliminating racial injustices."

By 1932, the *World*, which began as a weekly, had enough circulation to branch out as a daily. By this time, it had also founded the first chain of Black newspapers in America. At its height, the chain, known as Scott Syndicated Newspapers, owned papers in 50 cities throughout the nation. It was disbanded in 1970.

It was a *World* reporter, Harry S. McAlphin, who in 1942 became the first Black to join the White House press corps under F.D.R. His reports were syndicated to other Black newspapers.

In 1959, the *World* became the only Black organization to receive the Georgia State Chamber of Commerce's "Accolade of Appreciation" for the paper's economic contribution to the state. It was just another in a long history of firsts.

Margaret
1900-

Gone With the Wind made Atlanta a legend. Its characters, Scarlett O'Hara, Rhett Butler, Melanie and Ashley Wilkes passed into American folklore. And their creator, Margaret Mitchell, became a reluctant celebrity. To the rest of the nation, she came to represent Atlanta.

Indeed, Atlanta was in Margaret Mitchell's blood. She was born here in 1900 as her parents were. Her grandparents owned cotton plantations near Atlanta before there was an Atlanta.

The family was Southern to the core. The melodies that lulled Margaret to sleep as a child were Confederate ballads; her youthful reading included the "War Time Diary of a Georgia Girl" and other Civil War stories. As though they had happened yesterday, Confederate battles were refought at family gatherings.

"I was writing about an upheaval I'd known about when I was a small child," Margaret Mitchell wrote to a reviewer. "For I spent the Sunday afternoons of my girlhood sitting on the bony knees of Confederate veterans and the fat slick laps of old ladies who survived the war and reconstruction. And I heard them talk about friends who came through it all and friends who went under."

Gone With the Wind, in which all these strands came together, was written between 1926 and 1929, except for three chapters which were added later. In all, the book was 10 years in the writing, including months devoted to painstaking verification of the minutest historical details. During four of these years, the author was so crippled by arthritis it was feared she would never walk again.

Yet the book was published almost by accident. The pitying

Mitchell
1949

comment of a friend that Margaret "really wasn't the type who would write a successful book" spurred Miss Mitchell into rushing off and giving her partially completed manuscript to a visiting publisher.

Instant fame greeted the new novelist. For her and her husband, John R. Marsh, privacy became almost impossible to achieve, except by escaping into the countryside.

As Miss Mitchell wrote to a friend, "It sometimes seems to me that *Gone With the Wind* is not my book any longer; it is something about which the citizens are sensitive and sore at real and fancied slights and discriminations and are ready to fight at the drop of a hairpin."

When a rumor reached the city that the movie premiere might not be held in Atlanta, Miss Mitchell recounted in a letter, "Mayor Hartsfield announced to the press that this was the worst outrage since Sherman burned the town." In the end, His Honor prevailed, and the premiere was held in 1939 with great pomp and ceremony at the now-demolished Loews Grand Theatre on Peachtree Street.

Miss Mitchell was struck by a car and killed in 1949. She is buried in Oakland Cemetery near the graves of Confederate soldiers whose gallant defense of a lost cause she made known throughout the world.

Passages from Margaret Mitchell's letters are excerpted from: Richard Harwell, ed., *Margaret Mitchell's "Gone With The Wind" Letters 1936-1949* (New York: Macmillan Publishing Co., Inc., 1976). They are reprinted here by kind permission of Mr. Stephens Mitchell and Mr. Richard Harwell.

Joel Chandler Harris
1848-1908

"There is nothing striking about him — what strange habitations does genius choose among men!", a contemporary wrote after meeting Joel Chandler Harris. Yet ordinary Joe Harris, whose shyness made him retreat from any stranger, gave pleasure to strangers around the world through his plantation tales.

Millions of children have listened, as enthralled as the little boy sitting at Uncle Remus's knee, to the adventures of Brer Rabbit, Brer Fox, and the Tar-Baby narrated by Harris's fictional storyteller, the old slave, Uncle Remus.

Harris himself learnt many of the stories from slaves on the plantation where he lived as a youth; he picked up others from Black railroad workers in Atlanta after he moved here in 1876 to work for *The Atlanta Constitution*. Harris was meticulous in checking the authenticity of the stories, many of which were found to resemble both African and American-Indian folk tales, and in reproducing the exact speech of the plantation slaves.

It was said of Joe Harris, after his death, that no man since Abraham Lincoln had got nearer to the hearts of the whole people. His home, The Wren's Nest, named for a wren who made a nest in his mailbox, is open to the public at 1050 Gordon Street, S. W.

ACTION STATIONS

AM STATIONS

WAUC (550) — Black
WPLO (590) — Country
WRNG (680) — News-Talk
WSB (750) — Variety
WQXI (790) — Top Forty
WAEC (860) — Christian
WGST (920) — News
WKLS (970) — Album-Rock
WGUN (1010) — Religious
WCOB (1080) — Nostalgia
WGKA (1190) — Classical
WFOM (1230) — Top Forty
WTJH (1260) — Gospel
WCHK (1290) — Country
WXLL (1310) — Gospel
WIGO (1340) — Black
WLAW (1360) — Variety
WAOK (1380) — Black
WAVO (1420) — Religious
WDYX (1460) — Country
WYZE (1480) — Jazz Gospel
WDGL (1520) — Christian
WZAL (1540) — Top Forty
WYNX (1550) — Gospel
WSSA (1570) — Country
WACX (1600) — Country-Gospel

FM STATIONS

*WRAS (88.5) — Rock
WRFG (89.3) — Diversified
*WABE (90.1) — Educational-Classical
*WREK (91.1) — Progressive
WCLK (91.9) — Jazz-Black
*WZGC (92.9) — Top Forty
*WQXI (94.1) — Album-Rock
*WPCH (94.9) — Standards
WKLS (96.1) — Album-Rock
WSB (98.5) — Standards
*WLTA (99.7) — Popular
*WBIE (101.5) — Country
WGCO (102.3) — Country-Gospel
*WVEE (103.3) — Disco-Jazz
WCHK (105.5) — Country
* — Stereo

ON THE AIR

Major John S. Cohen, president and editor of *The Atlanta Journal*, brought Atlanta and the South their first commercial radio station, W S B, in 1922. Since then the airwaves have grown steadily more crowded. Forty stations now broadcast their messages to the metropolis.

There are stations for every taste: religious, ethnic, academic, musical, or intellectual. You can catch National Public Radio on WABE FM, classical music daytimes on WGKA, round-the-clock news on WGST, and "alternative" radio on WRFG.

WRFG — it stands for Radio Free Georgia — is a sort of survivor of the Sixties. It is non-commercial, relies on memberships, grants and luck to survive, and operates out of a decrepit studio in the Little Five Points area. WRFG's programming includes genuine bluegrass, non-commercial country music, public affairs reporting — including live broadcasts from the Butler Street Y's well-known Hungry Club — and even programs for the gay community. The station also offers a program of music from India at 8 PM on Fridays, and another of news and music in Spanish at the same time on Saturdays.

When you need to blow off steam, the station to turn to is WRNG — Ring Radio. It's a station that specializes in call-in programs, and you can hear the most surprising views expressed.

News is the focus of WGST. Events around the world are reported as they happen, 24 hours a day.

Turn to FM 90.1 for public radio, including the acclaimed news programs, "Morning Edition" at 7 a.m. and "All Things Considered" at 5 p.m.

The motley melodies of many kinds of music assail the ears as the dial is turned to other stations. The crashing beat of rock, the pickin' of country, the syncopation of jazz, the swing of big bands, the sweetness of the symphony — it's all on the air.

115

OF CARSON, COSELL, CRONKITE, & CAVETT

TV or not TV? That is the question most people face at the end of a long day.

If TV, what?

Eight local television stations offer Atlanta a choice of nonsense, news, or knowledge. Cable TV brings an added range of options.

Avenging angels and slinking celebrities represent the three commercial networks. ABC's affiliate is Channel 2, CBS's Channel 5, and NBC's Channel 11.

There's relief from the lather of soaps and the blather of game shows on Atlanta's two public television stations: Channel 8, a service of Georgia Public TV, and Channel 30, presented by the Atlanta and Fulton County public schools.

Playing to the business community, Channel 36 provides business and financial news, as well as continuous stock-price listings, weekdays from 10 a.m. to 5 p.m. At night and on weekends a mixture of entertainment, sport, and religious programming is offered.

Family entertainment is Channel 46's bag. A subsidiary of the Christian Broadcasting Network, the station also features several religious programs. It relays newscasts of the Independent Network News Service at 11:30 a.m. and 11 p.m.

Sport and old movies are the stock in trade of Channel 17, Ted Turner's "Superstation," which is broadcast by cable to the rest of the nation.

Cable television, recently introduced to Atlanta, opens up many other channels to the viewer. Indeed, Atlanta's sophisticated telecommunications industry is rapidly making the region a center of production for many cable networks.

In addition to Turner's Cable News Network, two other systems are based in the city. The Weather Channel, a 24-hour, live, continuous weather service, owned by John Coleman, the popular weatherman of ABC's "Good Morning America" program, recently commenced operations here. Westinghouse and ABC have also announced plans for a joint cable news service to be broadcast from Atlanta.

To hook up with your local cable system, contact your city or county government for information.

And chalk up another victim of the one-eyed monster.

THE SPACED-OUT NEWS STATION

Two years ago, it would have been hard to picture Atlanta as the center of a national and international news network. Yet that is what it became when a pioneering, all-news cable television system was launched here.

The spider weaving this intricate communications web is Ted Turner. Turner is known as many things: a champion yachtsman, owner of Atlanta's professional baseball and basketball teams, owner of WTBS, the self-styled "superstation," and "The Mouth of the South." His unique style, a combination of brash and dash, has even earned him a place in a comic strip. Turner was the model for Ashley Dashley III ("Ash to his friends") in the "Bloom County" cartoon syndicated to 83 newspapers.

But it is for none of these attributes that Turner wishes to be remembered.

Instead, he hankers to go down in history "as somebody who was successful in improving the flow of information to the American people."

His new 24-hour Cable News Network (CNN) is certainly the ideal opportunity to do this. And it could have the additional effect of making Turner one of the most influential men in America.

CNN began broadcasting in 1980. It provides round-the-clock live news coverage, beamed by satellite to affiliated cable television services throughout the nation.

CNN even has a young sister, CNN 2, that broadcasts brief news roundups on a 24-hour basis.

They are exciting ventures, brought to you by a man who is willing to put his money where his mouth is.

VIII

HEY, BIG SPENDERS!

Hogan

In the Heart of Atlanta

MINDING
THE
STORE

In Atlanta, weekends were made for merchandisers. Retailing is one of the fastest growing employment sectors in the metropolitan economy. The evidence is plain to see in the rapid spread of large regional shopping centers around the perimeter highway.

In a book of this type it is naturally impossible to name all the stores or even all the main shopping areas of Atlanta. Here we'll simply try and introduce you to certain types of specialty stores, to antique rows and other areas with a concentration of similar stores, and to some of the best places to bargain hunt.

A Who's Who of Atlanta Retailers

The godfather of Atlanta retailers is Rich's. The first Rich's store was opened at 36 Whitehall Street in 1867 by Morris L. Rich. Business prospered and the single store grew into a chain.

Rich's has given Atlanta a Christmas tradition — the annual lighting on Thanksgiving night of a giant Christmas tree atop its downtown store. Each year, the forests of the Southeast are combed for the perfect specimen. Found, it is carefully hauled to Atlanta and installed over the bridge connecting the two parts of the downtown store. Choirs selected from the best in Atlanta occupy the lighted galleries below the tree and pour out carols at the magical moment when the tree is lit. For the thousands of Atlantans who gather in the street below to watch, this joyous ceremony marks the start of the Christmas season.

Other noted Atlanta department store chains are Davison's (a subsidiary of Macy's, New York), J. P. Allen and Muse's.

The classiest shopping centers in Atlanta are both in Buckhead. Lenox Square, the oldest and most successful mall in the metropolitan area, caters to a mix of middle and upper-income folks. Phipps Plaza, diagonally opposite, serves

121

only the wealthiest; it's Atlanta's Fifth Avenue. Smaller centers patronized by the chic are Andrews Square, 56 East Andrews Drive in Buckhead, and Park Place, 4505 Ashford Dunwoody Road.

The Heart of Atlanta

The city's oldest shopping district is still one of its busiest and certainly one of its most fascinating. Variously referred to as the Heart of Atlanta or the South CBD, the area sandwiched between Marietta, Mitchell, Peachtree and Spring Streets downtown hums with vitality. Here small butcher shops, pawn shops, furniture stores, dime stores, fish markets, shoe and clothing stores jostle each other.

Fierce controversy rages over what will eventually become of this historic area. Over the years its clientele has changed; now, most customers are Black and many are poor. Marketing experts would sniff at such a formula for success; yet most businesses here are extremely profitable. Some developers, however, would like to see part of the area demolished to make way for a spanking new shopping center-office complex. Others would like to see it turned into an historic district. Still others would like to see it just spruced up. Which side wins is still to be decided.

Sweet Auburn

"Sweet Auburn! loveliest village of the plain," Oliver Goldsmith wrote in his poem, "The Deserted Village." This line was perhaps the inspiration for John Wesley Dobbs to apply the epithet to Atlanta's Auburn Avenue.

Auburn Avenue is the birthplace of Black enterprise in Atlanta, the street that nourished and gave birth to the city's long-established Black elite.

The concentration of Black businesses in this area was the result of racial segregation which squeezed them out of the White downtown. When the end of legal segregation in the 1960's opened up new areas for Black residence and investment, the economic vitality of Auburn Avenue began to suffer.

Today, Auburn Avenue is in decline, but efforts are being made to revive it by using the historic businesses that have remained in place as a catalyst. One of these is the Atlanta Life Insurance Company, the biggest Black-owned business in Atlanta and the second-largest Black-owned insurance company in the nation. The company operates in 12 states with assets approaching $100 million. Other significant landmarks on Auburn Avenue are the half-century old *Atlanta Daily World*, Citizen's Trust Bank, the sixth largest Black-owned bank in the U.S., Mutual Federal Savings and Loan Association, and the Martin Luther King Center for Social Change.

A printed guide to Auburn Avenue, the *Sweet Auburn Walking Tour*, is available from the city's Department of Planning (tel.: 658-6306).

METRO ATLANTA'S MAJOR MALLS

Belvedere Plaza
cnr. Memorial and Columbia Drs.
Decatur

Cobb Center
2200 S. Cobb Dr., S.E. (cnr. Pat Mell Rd.)
Smyrna

Columbia Mall
3604 Memorial Dr. (cnr. Columbia Dr.)
Decatur

Cumberland Mall
U.S. 41 at I-285 W
Cobb

Greenbriar Mall
2841 Greenbriar Pkwy., S.W.
Atlanta

Lenox Square
3393 Peachtree Rd., N.E. (cnr. Lenox Rd.)
Atlanta

North DeKalb Mall
2144 Lawrenceville Hwy. (cnr. N. Druid Hills Rd.)
Decatur

Northlake Mall
4800 Briarcliff Rd., N.E. (at I-285 E)
DeKalb

Perimeter Mall
4400 Ashford-Dunwoody Rd., N.E.
DeKalb

Phipps Plaza
3500 Peachtree Rd., N.E.
Atlanta

Shannon Mall
I-85 at Jonesboro Rd./
Union City exit

South DeKalb Mall
2845 Candler Rd. (at I-20 E)
Decatur

Southlake Mall
Ga. 54 at I-75 S
Morrow

CHEAP
THRILLS

The big events the Atlanta bargain-hunter saves for are the warehouse sales held periodically by Rich's and its major rival, Davison's. Goods from nearly every department can be found at reduced prices. Remember, though, that the early bird gathers the worm.

If you can't wait for a sale, Atlanta is liberally provided with outlet stores. Some of these are linked to the textile and apparel factories that have migrated to the South.

In addition, J. C. Penney and Sears operate a number of catalog surplus stores throughout the metropolitan area. These stores sell catalog returns, over-stocks and some damaged items.

Factory To You

You can also save by buying directly from a factory, especially in mens-wear. The Arrow shirt factory operates a store in East Point and another in Austell near Six Flags; ladies' blouses are first quality, men's shirts mainly "seconds." You can also buy men's suits, coats and pants direct from the factory at Walton Clothes on South Cobb Parkway in Smyrna, and from Zeeman Man-ufacturing Company's stores in Chamblee, Fulton Industrial Boulevard and Lithonia. Store addresses and telephone numbers are listed in the telephone directory.

Home Furnishings

If you have connections with an interior decorator, you may be able to gain access to Atlanta's two giant furniture wholesalers, Charles S. Martin Distributing Company and Southeast Wholesale Furniture Company, or to the Atlanta Decorative Arts Center, with its many dealer's showrooms open only to the trade.

If you ain't connected, you could take a trip to North Carolina, where in towns like High Point, Hickory, Thomasville, and many others, furniture makers display and sell their wares at prices generally lower than you'll find elsewhere.

If neither option seems feasible, don't despair. There are still bargains to be had. The warehouses of Designhouse International and House of Denmark sell discontinued items of Danish furniture to the public at savings. Both warehouses are on the I-85 access road near Jimmy Carter Boulevard in Norcross. For contemporary furniture, try the Storehouse clearance center in Buckhead. Levitz also has clearance centers in its two huge stores in Doraville and College Park.

Carpeting

Dalton, a little town off I-75 in Northwest Georgia, makes big claims — to being the Carpet Capital of the world, in fact. You can buy carpet direct from mill stores here, but experts advise you to decide what you want first and to make a few calls to manufacturers to compare prices before you come.

Barter is Better

John wants to learn to play the piano. John mows lawns. Jane teaches piano. Jane wants her lawn mowed. Will John and Jane ever meet?

In a less perfect world, perhaps not. But in Atlanta, quite possibly. The Atlanta Network is an organization formed specifically to enable individuals to barter service for service.

The Network bills itself as a "unique, non-profit, educational organization that enables you to meet people in and around your neighborhood who want to teach, learn, or share common interests with you." Through the Network, individuals can exchange skills or get in touch with others who enjoy attending concerts, visiting art galleries, or discussing such topics as Hermeneutics, Nero Wolfe mysteries, and Black Holes.

There is a $15 annual membership fee. Further information can be obtained from The Atlanta Network, P. O. Box 14432, Atlanta, Georgia 30324 (tel.: 876-8888).

The Best

Here's a concise list of shopping centers with heavy concentrations of outlet and discount stores. Try them — you'll like them!

Atlanta Trade Center
Commerce Drive, S.W.
Atlanta

An assemblage of distributor's warehouses and retail shops makes this a good place to visit if you're in the market for clothes. You'll find shoes, handbags, coats, dresses, jeans and slacks, even double-knit fabrics in this group of outlets. Many are open to the public only on Fridays (all day) and Saturday mornings, and most only accept cash.

Take I-20 W to the Fulton Industrial Boulevard exit, turn left onto Commerce Drive from the Boulevard.

Belmont Plaza Shopping Center
South Atlanta Road
Smyrna

This center is virtually a collection of outlet stores. It includes both Sears and Penney's surplus stores, as well as linen, clothing and shoe outlets, and a salvage store.

Bargains

Northeast Plaza Shopping Center
3300 block, Buford Highway
Doraville

Another great collection of outlet stores, including a Penney's, Loehmann's — famed for its cut-rate prices on women's designer clothes — an imports warehouse, and a shoe outlet.

Pinetree Plaza Shopping Center
5100 block, Buford Highway
Doraville

A Sears surplus store anchors this center, which also contains a discount ladies' clothing store, a salvage store, and a fine-china outlet.

Shoppers' Mall
4166 Buford Highway, N. E.
Doraville

Anchored by a Marshall's store, this center features a number of discount outlets, including Tuesday Morning.

ATLANTA'S ANTIQUE ROWS

A booth in a local flea market used to display this warning: "$1 charge if we have to listen to how your grandmother used to have one."

Well, nearly anything your grandmother might have had is likely to be available today from one of the hundreds of antique dealers in Atlanta. The region is chock-full of flea markets, auction houses, malls and stores jammed with "antiques" of variable antiquity. Antique fairs, like that at Crabapple, draw treasure-hunters in droves.

Here's a guide to some of the places where clusters of dealers can be found. They're fun to visit even if you're just browsing. Individual stores are listed in the yellow pages.

Location	Hours
Atlanta Antique Market 5360 Peachtree Industrial Blvd. Chamblee	F.-Sun., 11 am - 7 pm

Successor to the original Atlanta Flea Market on Piedmont Road, this 80,000 square foot market features antiques, collectibles, accessories and art.

Location	Hours
Chamblee Antique Row Broad St./Peachtree Rd. area	M.-Sat., 10 am - 5 pm Sun., noon - 5 pm

Some 35 stores are grouped around this intersection. Hours may vary from store to store.

Take I-285 N, turn south on Peachtree Industrial Boulevard, left on Broad Street.

The Crabapple Antique Fair

Elco's Georgia Antique Fair
4150 I-75 South Expressway
College Park

Second weekend every month.
Sat.-Sun., 9 am - 6 pm

Scores of dealers exhibit collectibles at this huge flea market.

Take I-75 S to Central Ave./Old Dixie Rd. exit. Go south one mile on Old Dixie Rd. (U.S. 3/19/41), turn right on College Park Rd.

Flea Market at Forest Park
4855 Jonesboro Rd.

F.-Sat., 10 am - 9 pm
Sun., noon - 6 pm

Some 200 booths selling merchandise of all types make up this indoor market.

Take I-75 S to the Farmers' Market exit; turn left onto Ga. 331 then right on Ga. 54 (Jonesboro Rd.)

Gold's Antique Mall
1149 Lee St., S.W.

Sat., 10 am - 6 pm
Sun., 1 - 6 pm

Thirty-two dealer spaces are located in this auction house.

Great Southeast Flea Market
4343 Northeast Expressway
Doraville

F.-Sat., noon - 9:30 pm
Sun., noon - 7 pm

One of Atlanta's largest and newest markets, located on the access road near the intersection of I-85 and I-285.
Take Exit 36 off I-85.

Howell Mill Antique Mall
1189 Howell Mill Rd., N.W.

M. - Sat., 10 am - 5 pm

Several dealers are clustered here just north of 14th Street.

Peachtree Flea Market
3167 Peachtree Rd., N.E.

Th. - Sat., 10 am - 7 pm
Sun., noon - 7 pm

Some 100 booths located in the heart of Buckhead.

Peachtree Street
Pershing Point — Peachtree Hills Ave.

Antique stores are scattered at intervals along this stretch of Peachtree. Most are closed Sunday.

Roswell/Crabapple

Nineteen antique shops are located along the Atlanta Street-Canton Street-Crabapple Road-Mayfield Road strip north of the Chattahoochee River in Fulton County. Begin your journey on Roswell Road off I-285 and you'll reach your destination. Many are open Sundays.

Smyrna Antique Row
Atlanta Rd.

Several stores are clustered in the area centered on the intersection of Atlanta Road and Concord Road.

Vinings Area
Paces Ferry Road/Mountain Ave.

There's a fair grouping of antique stores in this area. Many are closed Mondays.

Architectural Antiques

Store	Telephone	Hours
Bygone Era 4783 Peachtree Road	458-3016	M.-Sat., 9 am - 6 pm
Frogg Restorations 337 Georgia Ave., S.E.	627-5891	T.,W., 3 - 5 pm Th.-Sat., 10 am - 5 pm
Red Baron Antiques 3264 Peachtree Rd., N.E.	237-9338	M.-Sat., 9 am - 6 pm
The Wrecking Bar 292 Moreland Ave., N.E.	525-0468	M.-Sat., 9 am - 5 pm

THE BIBLIOPHILE'S ATLANTA

Only the true book-lover can understand the appeal of books and the instinct, almost the compulsion, to possess them. And perhaps only he can fully understand what the great English novelist, E. M. Forster, meant when he wrote of the books in his library, "It is very pleasant to sit with them in the firelight for a couple of minutes, not reading, not even thinking, but aware that they, with their accumulated wisdom and charm, are waiting to be used." It is to addicts of this type that this section is addressed.

The great events in the Atlanta book lover's year are the annual used book sales conducted by Brandeis University supporters and by the Atlanta branch of the American Association of University Women. The Brandeis sale is usually held in May under a marquee in the parking lot of Phipps Plaza in Buckhead, and the AAUW's in the third week of September in Lenox Square.

Here's a guide to dealers in new and old books in Atlanta. It excludes the many religious bookstores as well as those specializing in the metaphysical and occult; you'll find both groups listed in the yellow pages.

Books in Print

The two major chains, B. Dalton and Waldenbooks, are well represented in Atlanta. You'll find one of them in most of the regional malls. Smaller chains with stores in Atlanta are Brentano's and Cole's.

While the chains generally specialize in best sellers and the most popular categories of books, independent bookstores tend to carry a wider range of books, though many specialize in one area. Here's a list of some of the best independents.

Store	Telephone

Ansley Mall Book Store   875-6492
1544 Piedmont Ave., N.E.

Ardmore Book End   256-4203
5964 Roswell Road
(Hammond Square Shopping Center)

Book Rack Plus Inc.   233-1611
2581 Piedmont Road, N.E.
(Broadview Plaza)

    This store specializes in books on antiques and metaphysics.

Business Book Center   266-2716
3384 Peachtree Road, N.E.

    Materials on management training, career development and finance.

Charis Books   524-0304
419 Moreland Ave., N.E.

    Children's books and books on women's issues a specialty.

Cokesbury   525-0501
72 Broad St., N.E.

    Emphasis on religious books.

Doubleday Book Shop   892-0403
Colony Square

Dunwoody Book Center   393-0902
5552 Chamblee-Dunwoody Rd.
(Dunwoody Hall Shopping Center)

Hale's Books   977-9456
1315 Johnson Ferry Rd., N.E.
Marietta
(Merchants Walk Shopping Center)

133

Oxford Book Store   262-3332
2341-C Peachtree Rd., N.E.
(Peachtree Battle Shopping Center)

One of the biggest and one of the best. A coffee shop above is an added attraction.

Rizzoli International Bookstore   688-9065
328 Omni International

Not really an independent, but carries the best selection of books and records in other languages and of books on the arts.

Roswell Book Store   992-8485
100 Norcross St.
Roswell
(Canterbury Plaza)

Tall Tales Bookshop   636-2498
2999 N. Druid Hills Rd., N.E.
(Toco Hills Shopping Center)

Williamsburg Bookstore   633-4151
2777 Clairmont Rd., N.E.

General, with emphasis on childrens books and records.

Out of Print

"As for the first edition craze," wrote E. M. Forster, "I place it next door to stamp collecting — I can say no less."
In spite of Forster's disapproval, which was based on his conviction that books should be savored for what they say, not for their bindings or their date, many people do enjoy the thrill of rarity. Not all the dealers listed below cater to this appetite — some simply stock used books and old faithfuls that have gone out of print — but all are worth visiting.

Store   **Telephone**

Arnold's Archives   394-2665
5519-D Chamblee-Dunwoody Rd.
(Dunwoody Village Shopping Center)
        &

1579 N. Decatur Rd.   377-2665

This store sells new books, but its specialty is signed first editions and limited editions.

Hound Dog Press Book Shop   292-2093
4285 Memorial Dr., Suite A
Decatur

This store specializes in southern Appalachia, Georgia, and the South and offers book searches for out of print titles.

Old Book Scout   257-1012
4175 Roswell Rd.

Book searches are a specialty here.

Old New York Book Shop   881-1285
1069 Juniper St., N.E.

Some 30,000 titles are jammed into this old house in the Midtown area. They cover just about every subject. If you're simply browsing, allow a couple of hours; there's even free coffee to keep up your strength.

Woolf's Den Books   233-8727
3625 Peachtree Rd., N.E.

This store offers a general selection and book search service.

Yesteryear Book Shop   237-0163
256 E. Paces Ferry Rd., N.E.

The emphasis here is on Americana, especially the South and Georgia, and on first editions.

Free Enterprise, Cabbagetown style

THE
CONNED
CONSUMER

You began with a polite request. Gradually, your calls and letters grew more and more insistent, then demanding, then plain angry. Still your fixed faucet continued to drip, the rattle in your car rattled on, the mail-ordered item failed to arrive. Now you're furious and frustrated.

What's your next move? Give up? Go to court? Call Channel 5 or Channel 11's Mr. Fixit and hope your problem is one of the small number selected for investigation? None of the above?

Many people reject the court option. It seems too cumbersome and expensive. But it's often cheaper and easier than you think. And the "none of the above" category offers some pretty interesting alternatives as well. Here are some avenues you might explore.

Tel-Law: A Guide Through the Legal System

First, it often helps to know what your legal rights are. Tel-Law, a community service project of the Atlanta Bar Association, is a means of providing the public with general information about specific legal problems without the obscurities and at no cost. This information is available simply by calling Tel-Law (tel.: 577-4357) and requesting by number the playing of a tape on the subject in which you are interested.

Topics covered relate both to criminal and civil matters. Subjects discussed include how to deal with a traffic ticket, what you should know about being a witness, parents' liability for damage done by their children, adoption, what to do about noisy neighbors, divorce and child support, bankruptcy, social security, and consumers' rights, among many others.

The service operates Mondays to Fridays, from 9 am to noon and from 1:30 to 4:30 pm.

137

The Small-Claims Court

The small-claims court has been called "the bargain basement of the legal system." Its advantages are two: you don't need a lawyer; and the cost is minimal.

There is a standard procedure for filing a small claim in most jurisdictions. Generally, the person who files the claim (the plaintiff) must be an individual, not a corporation. The claim must be filed in the county in which the person or corporation who is being sued (the defendant) resides. The defendant has 45 days from the date on which notice of the claim is served on him by an officer of the court in which to respond. If the defendant does not respond within that time, judgment is usually automatically entered for the plaintiff, who thus wins his case.

If the defendant contests the claim, the plaintiff may appear in person, without a lawyer, to prove to the judge that he has a valid claim. He should bring proof if possible, for example, of how much the merchandise was worth, and may call witnesses if he wishes. However, the essence of small-claims proceedings is that the procedure is simple and the plaintiff can make his case in plain language; legal jargon is discouraged.

The maximum amount of the claim that can be heard in a small claims court varies with the jurisdiction, as do costs. In Fulton, the plaintiff is not permitted to use a lawyer; in most other jurisdictions, however, use of lawyers is optional. In Clayton, small claims are handled through Justices of the Peace.

County	Max. Claim	Telephone
Clayton	$500	471-2151
Cobb	$300	429-3625
DeKalb	Open	371-2261
Fulton	$300	572-2101

Mediation: The Neighborhood Justice Center

The Neighborhood Justice Center aims to settle disputes through mediation between the warring parties. It receives funding from both public and private sources. Generally, the problems the Center attempts to resolve involve long-standing relationships, such as between employer and employee, landlord and tenant, consumer and contractor, husband and wife, or neighbor and neighbor.

When a problem is submitted to the Center, either by an individual or a public agency, a mediator notifies the person whose actions are the subject of complaint. He is informed that the complainant has the option of taking the matter to court, and is invited to agree to let the Center mediate the dispute instead. Some disputes can be settled over the telephone, others require meetings

138

with the mediator. When agreement is reached, both parties are asked to put it in writing and sign it.

The Center does not provide legal advice (and disputes submitted need not be based on a legally enforceable claim), nor does it provide counseling. Its offices are at 1118 Euclid Avenue, N.E., Atlanta (tel.: 523-8236).

The Governor's Office of Consumer Affairs (OCA)

Yes, the Governor does care whether you get ripped off or not: this office exists to prove it. It has three purposes: to investigate consumer complaints and enforce laws prohibiting unfair and deceptive business practices, to educate the public about sensible consumer habits, and to expose con-artists and their works.

If you have a complaint about a company with which you have been doing business, your first step should be to attempt to resolve it yourself. If that fails, OCA investigators can investigate your problem, suggest some remedies, and, if you have been a victim of an unfair or deceptive business practice, obtain an injunction forbidding the practice. Under the Fair Business Practices Act, there's a hefty penalty of $25,000 for firms violating such injunctions.

The most visible sign of OCA's activities is the state information and referral system, *Tie-Line* (tel.: 656-7000 in Atlanta, 1-800-282-5808 in the rest of Georgia.) Tie-Line investigates consumer complaints, and provides referrals to state regulatory agencies, such as those overseeing insurance companies, and to professional and licensing boards.

Alternatively, you can write to the Office of Consumer Affairs, 225 Peachtree Street, N.E., Suite 400, Atlanta, Georgia 30303. Remember to state actions you have already taken, and enclose copies of any supporting documents, such as checks.

The Ag Consumer Line

The Georgia Department of Agriculture regulates all food processors in the state. It ensures that all food sold here meets the department's standards for quality and cleanliness, and that the labeling of processed food accurately reflects the ingredients.

The department also calibrates all scales in Georgia, whether they are used to weigh food or precious metals. It regulates and tests antifreeze and the octane ratings of gasoline sold here.

The Ag Consumer Line (tel.: 656-3645 in metro Atlanta, 1-800-282-5852 in the rest of the state) is a hotline for consumers who feel they have been shortchanged. All complaints are investigated by the Department's inspectors. Disgruntled customers may also write to: Consumer Services, Room 300, Georgia Department of Agriculture, Capitol Square, Atlanta, Ga. 30334.

IX

FOOD, GLORIOUS FOOD

Municipal Market

THE MARKETS
OF
ATLANTA

The food markets of Atlanta range from the 146-acre State Farmers' Market in Forest Park to the friendly Saturday gatherings of local farmers in Alpharetta. You can find everything from fresh produce to whole pigs, from fish to fowl.

The *DeKalb Farmers' Market*, (640 Medlock Road, Decatur, tel.: 325-8730) which is privately owned, is perhaps the nicest produce market in Atlanta. It's lively, varied, well-priced and fun. Most of the market is devoted to vegetables and fruit, but you can also buy fresh fish, cheese, and poultry here. It is open every day.

Other markets impress by their size or variety of tenants. For example, the *State Farmers' Market*, opened in 1959, is said to trade $100,000,000 worth of produce every year. It serves farmers, wholesalers and the general public.

The State Farmers' Market is arranged in two sections. In the Farmers' Shed area, farmers rent stalls and sell directly to the public. Prices and quality vary, so shop around. In the second part of the market, ten buildings, covering more than half a million square feet in area, provide space for wholesalers who sell in bulk. Here you'll find goodies ranging through the alphabet from A for Anice to Z for Zucchini. If you're afraid no-one will kiss you at Christmas, buy a sprig of mistletoe from the dealer in Stall 35 and sway the odds in your favor.

In Building K you'll find the meat market. It's open to the public and sells all types of fresh meat as well as frozen fish and poultry. You can also buy a variety of cheeses, smoked sausages, ham and bacon, and frozen vegetables.

Atlanta's *Municipal Market* is the oldest in the city. It has served the people of Atlanta for some seven decades. The present building was erected in 1923, replacing an open-air market which had long been held on the same site. The Municipal Market is owned by the City of Atlanta.

The visitor's first impression is of being surrounded by portions of the pig's anatomy that he did not know existed, at least not as edible items. Pig processors say they use every part of the pig but the squeak, and every usable part can be seen at the Municipal Market. There are disembodied pigs' ears in heaps, pigs' feet, pigs' snouts, pigs' tails, and pigs' entrails — chitlin's, they call them here. There's even a Pig Man, W. C. Hardeman, who believes in the whole hog, and sells it too.

[For a fascinating account of the uses to which the unlikelier parts of the pig were put in rural Georgia, consult Chapter Nine of Harry Crews' remarkable book, *A Childhood: The Biography of a Place* (New York: Harper and Row, 1978.)]

If you've a fancy for rabbit, you can find it at Roy's Seafood, along with squid, steamed crab, lobster tails, frogs' legs, turtle-meat and other delicacies.

The Market also boasts an excellent cheese stand, butchers, poulterers, produce stands and such unlikely items as wigs, insurance and religious tokens.

Farm Fresh

One of the nicest ways of stocking your larder is to gather the harvest yourself.

A number of farmers in the rural counties every year permit city folks to gather fruit from their orchards and pay for what is picked. A listing of farms in the metropolitan area where pickin' is possible is published every year in the Georgia Department of Agriculture's Farmers and Consumers Market Bulletin (tel.: 656-3682). Even Christmas trees can be cropped.

Atlanta also has one of the only three certified dairies in the nation producing raw milk — milk that is not pasteurized. It was founded by Mr. R. L. Mathis in 1917 and is still family owned and operated. Mathis milk, cheese, kefir, and cream is sold at the Mathis dairy store, and at health food outlets, or you can have it delivered to your door.

Atlanta's Very Cooperative Extension Services

The Cooperative Extension Services offered by each county in Georgia are an excellent resource for the home gardener. They provide advice on every aspect of gardening — from selecting plant varieties best suited to conditions in Atlanta to the treatment of disease and insect infestations. A variety of courses for homemakers are also offered.

Best of all, these services are free!

To contact the Extension Service in your county, call:

County	Telephone
Cobb	422-2320, ext. 211/315

Clayton	478-9911, ext. 340
DeKalb	371-2821
Fulton	572-3261
Gwinnett	963-1480

Market Facts

State Farmers' Market
16 Forest Parkway
Forest Park
Telephone: 366-6910
Farmers' Shed Area: M-Sun., 24 hours.
Meat Market: M-Sun., 8 am - 5 pm
  Take I-75 South to Forest Parkway exit.

Municipal Market
209 Edgewood Avenue, SE
Telephone: 659-1665

M-Th., 8 am - 5:45 pm
F-Sat., 8 am - 6:45 pm
Closed Sun.

Alpharetta Farmers' Market
Wills Road
Alpharetta
Telephone: 393-4670

Sat., 8:30 - 6 pm. Early shopping is advised for this informal market. Summer only.
  Take U.S. 19 to Wills Road. Market is held in Wills Park.

Can You Do The Can-Can?

There are those in the hills of Appalachia who swear that food put up when the dark side of the moon turns earthward will spoil, that canning when the moon is in Virgo is an invitation to disaster, that pickling must never be attempted before the fourth day of the new moon and then only under the influence of Aries, Gemini or Cancer.

You can call this folklore or superstition, wise or witless. But if you wish to store summer's harvest to warm you over winter, and whether you abide by the rules of the hillfolk or not, public canneries in Atlanta make it easier to put up your own vegetables, fruits, juices, meats, poultry, lard or crackling.

One of these canneries is located in the State Farmers' Market. The other is operated by the DeKalb County Cooperative Extension Service; DeKalb residents get preference but anyone may use this facility.

At both canneries, the customer brings her own produce, prepares it, and washes up. Assistance is always available if you need it. The dangerous processes — blanching, sealing, and pressure-cooking — are done for you by cannery experts. Modest charges are made for the cans. DeKalb's cannery will also hickory-smoke meat; make an appointment to arrange for all meat processing here.

Cannery	Hours	Telephone
DeKalb Ext. Service 3590 Kensington Rd. (cnr. Camp Rd.) Decatur	Three days/week, 8 am-5 pm	294-7449
State Farmers' Market 16 Forest Parkway Forest Park	July - Sept. M. & Th., 2-10 pm Tu., W., Sat., 9 am - 5 pm	366-6910

Storing the Harvest, DeKalb Cannery

JUST
BE
NATURAL

There are scores of health food stores in Atlanta. You'll find a pretty complete list in the Yellow Pages under "Health Food Products."

In addition to these commercial operations, a number of non-profit cooperative food stores serve the needs of those who believe that bran makes brawn and brain.

A coop is essentially a food-store owned by its patrons. Members pay a small fee to join, but work at the coop can often be substituted for cash payment. Since coops buy food in bulk and operate on a non-profit basis, members benefit from lower prices; they also have a vote in the running of the organization. You don't have to be a member to buy at a coop, but members obtain special discounts.

The coops of Atlanta are oriented toward natural foods. They generally sell a variety of grains, flours and rices in bulk or packaged, organically-grown produce, cold-pressed oils, herbs, cheeses, raw milk, yogurt, natural juices and sometimes even natural soaps and cosmetics.

Here is a list of the coops of Atlanta.

Sevananda
431 Moreland Avenue, NE
Tel.: 681-2831
M.-Sun., 11 am - 7:30 pm

Life Grocery Store, Inc.
961 Roswell St.
(in Sears parking lot, near fire station)
Marietta

Tel.: 427-5454
M.-Sat., 10 am - 7 pm

Kudzu Coop
Old Masonic Lodge
456 Cherokee Avenue
Grant Park
Tel.: 522-5015
M.-F., 11 am - 7 pm
Sat., 10 am - 4 pm

Magnolia Co-op Warehouse
1081 Memorial Drive, S.E. (basement)
Tel.: 523-4886

This is a warehouse selling natural foods in bulk, primarily to coops. Buying clubs formed by friends, neighbors or church groups also have access to this service. Order goods by number from a product list for pick-up on specified days.

FOREIGN FODDER

Atlanta, as we have seen, has a diverse population drawn from many parts of the world. And a surprisingly large number of people make a living catering to their eating habits.

In this section we'll tell you the best places to find ethnic and gourmet foodstuffs. In addition, some of the larger supermarkets, like Ogletrees, offer a variety of hard-to-find delicacies in their foreign-food departments.

Chinese and Oriental

Asian Trading Company, Ltd.
2581 Piedmont Road (Broadview Plaza)
Tel.: 266-0362

M.-Sat., 10 am - 8 pm
Sun., 11 am - 5 pm

Chinatown Grocery
2743 LaVista Road
Tel.: 321-3452

M.-Sat., 10:30 am - 7:30 pm
Sun., 1 to 5 pm

Dah-Tung Trading Company
659 Ethel St.
Tel.: 873-2066

Specialty: Freshly-made noodles

M-Sat., 10:30 am - 6:30 pm

Tung-Fong, Inc.
Ansley Square, Piedmont Rd.
Tel.: 876-6568

M.-Sun., 11:30 am - 6:30 pm

150

Greek and Gourmet

Happy Herman's
2299 Cheshire Bridge Road
Tel.: 321-3012

M.-Sat., 9 am - 10:30 pm
Sun., 9 am - 8:45 pm
&

204 Johnson Ferry Road
Sandy Springs
Tel.: 256-3354

M.-Th., 9 am - 10 pm
F.-Sat., 9 am - 11 pm
Sun., 9 am - 9 pm

Indian

International House of Spices
6654 Riverdale Plaza, Ga. 85
Riverdale
Tel.: 991-0110

M.-Sun., 10:30 am - 8:30 pm

Mira Enterprises
2376 Shallowford Terrace
Tel.: 455-8856

M.-F., 12:30 - 7:30 pm
Sat.-Sun., noon - 6 pm

Sapna Enterprise
2109 N. Decatur Rd.
Tel.: 329-1610

Tu.-F., 1 - 8 pm
Sat., Sun., 11:30 am - 7 pm

Jewish/Kosher

Arthur's Kosher Meat Market
2166 Briarcliff Road, N.E. (cnr. LaVista)
Tel.: 634-6881

M.-Th., 7 am - 6 pm
F., 7 am - 5 pm

Bernie's Kosher Meats
2345-3 Cheshire Bridge Road, N.E.
(Cheshire Square Shopping Center)
Tel.: 325-1559

M.-Th., 8 am - 5:30 pm
Fri., 8 am - 4 pm

Fred's Delicatessen and
Kosher Meats
1403 North Highland Avenue,
Tel.: 876-1029

M.-Th., 8 am - 6 pm
Fri., 8 am - 4 pm
Sun., 8:30 am - 4 pm

Goldberg and Son
4383 Roswell Road, N.E.
Tel.: 256-3751

Tu.-Fr., 9 am - 7 pm
Sat., 8 am - 7 pm
Sun., 8 am - 5 pm

The Royal Bagel
1544 Piedmont Avenue, N.E.
Tel.: 876-3512
&
6066 Sandy Springs Cir., N.E.
Tel.: 255-2299

Tu.-Sat., 7:30 am - 5 pm
Sun., 7 am - 3 pm

Latin American

Diaz Market
106 6th Street, N.E.
Tel: 872-0928
&
368 5th Street, N.E.
Tel.: 874-8641
&
755 Ponce de Leon Avenue, N.E.
Tel.: 875-6568
&
10 King Circle, N.E.
Tel.: 233-0182

M.-Sat., 9 am - 9 pm
Sun., 9 am - 6 pm

Rinconcito Latino
2581 Piedmont Road
(Broadview Plaza on
Marion Road side)
Tel.: 231-2329

M.-Sat., 9 am - 8 pm
Sun., 10 am - 5 pm

Middle Eastern

George's Delicatessen
1041 North Highland Avenue, N.E.
Tel.: 881-9397

M.F., 10:30 am - midnight
Sat., 9:30 am - 7 pm

Middle East Baking Co.
4000-B Pleasantdale Rd.
Tel.: 448-9190

M.-Sat., 9 am - 5 pm

Thai/Filipino

Lim's Oriental Gifts and Food
4887 Memorial Drive
Stone Mountain (Rockmore Plaza)
Tel.: 296-6106

M.-Sat., 10:30 am - 7 pm

X

THE OUTDOORS
AT
YOUR DOORSTEP

Rex Mill, Clayton County

STAY AND SEE
(OR SNIFF)
GEORGIA

This chapter introduces the reader to the outdoors at his doorstep: to parks, hiking trails, watersports, and hunting and fishing spots within an hour's drive of Atlanta, and often much closer than that. Some are actually within the city limits.

By arbitrarily restricting the scope of this section to the 15-county metropolitan area, we have obviously left untouched the many beautiful natural areas in the North Georgia mountains, along Georgia's golden coastline, and in the state's interior reaches. Happily, information on these regions is readily available from a number of sources.

Excellent color brochures and booklets describing *scenic and historic areas and outdoor activities* in all parts of the state are published free by the Georgia Bureau of Industry and Trade, Tourist Division, P. O. Box 1776, Atlanta, Georgia 30301 (tel.: 656-3590).

Guides to Georgia's *state parks* can be obtained free from the Georgia Department of Natural Resources, Parks and Historic Sites Division, 270 Washington Street, SW, Atlanta, Georgia 30334 (tel.: 656-3530).

For free information on *national parks* in Georgia and the Southeast, contact the National Park Service, Public Information Section, 75 Spring Street, SW, Atlanta, Georgia 30303 (tel.: 221-5187).

Information on *national forests* and *unspoiled wilderness areas* in Georgia and the Southeast can be obtained from the U. S. Forest Service, 1720 Peachtree Road, NW, Atlanta, Georgia 30309 (tel.: 881-2384).

The Georgia Travel Machine

In Georgia, the armchair traveller can experience the ultimate trip. If he can muster up the energy to visit the Georgia Welcome Center at Hartsfield International Airport he need go no further.

Technically, the Center is located midway between the airport's baggage claim areas. But in the imagination it wafts the visitor all over Georgia.

Here a computer-controlled movie presentation combines sights, sounds, temperatures and even smells from every region of the state: it's almost as good as being there.

As the North Georgia mountains undulate before you, you'll feel the air grow cooler and the scent of pine drift through the air. In Atlanta, you'll sniff peach blossoms. As you approach South Georgia, you'll grow warmer and the earthy smell of the soil will fill your nostrils. Finally, an increase in humidity and the bracing aroma of salty seas will introduce you to the Georgia coastline. Ah!

Hold tight — and have fun!

IN
THE
BEGINNING

In the beginning, there were violent movements beneath the earth's crust that determined the physical structure of Atlanta — even, perhaps, the collision of continental landmasses whose ripple effects created a long fault zone on Atlanta's western border.

But Atlanta's surface features were shaped, not by cataclysmic upheavals, but by the effect of millions of years of weathering by wind and water.

As you hike Atlanta's wooded trails, climb its rocky prominences, and raft its swirling streams, ponder the natural forces that produced them.

If you take I-285 West to where it crosses the Chattahoochee River, near the site of the former Chattahoochee Brick Company, and walk down to the river south of the expressway, you will notice an area where white rock is overlaid by a layer of grey stone. That combination, says Robert L. Atkins, a geologist with the Georgia Geologic Survey, is a result of the movement of the earth's surface that occurred when the Brevard Fault Zone was formed hundreds of millions of years ago.

Geologists speculate that the Fault may have been caused by a collision between the two "plates" on which the African and North American continents float that crumpled the earth's crust.

The course of the Chattahoochee roughly marks the line of the Fault Zone, and as you float downstream between the cliffs of the Palisades section, you'll see signs of the rock types that are characteristic of the fault — types that are different north and south of the river.

Heat and pressure deep in the earth's core also played their part in determining Atlanta's geological structure, creating banded rocks like the Lithonia Gneiss of which Arabia Mountain in DeKalb County is formed.

Such crushing forces may explain why there are no fossils in the Atlanta

157

area, even though fossils of plants and primitive animals are to be found in northwest Georgia and the Georgia coast.

Atlanta's Stone Mountains

Less old are granites like Stone Mountain and Panola Mountain. Stone Mountain is composed mainly of light-colored muscovite granite, Panola of darker biotite. Stone Mountain is often described — by Atlantans, at least — as the largest granite outcrop in the world. That's not true, according to Atkins. It's no more than an erosional remnant, he says.

In fact, we see Stone Mountain today because some 25 million years of erosion by wind and water have removed the layers of soil that once covered it and other features of the Atlanta landscape. Stone Mountain, like Kennesaw and Panola, may have survived because the rock of which it is composed was more resistant to erosion than the surrounding material.

The process by which rainwater, both with its force and its acidic content, can break down rock is still visible today. Visitors who take the guided hikes up Panola Mountain will have the evidence and process explained to them as they tramp its rocky slopes.

Rivers have also helped carve the Atlanta landscape. Atlanta is drained by three rivers: the beautiful Chattahoochee, the Flint, with its head waters near Hartsfield Airport, and the South River, which flows into the Altamaha. These rivers and their tributaries, over millions of years, dissolved and washed away the layers of soil covering the topography of Atlanta, and carried the silts and sediments south to form the Georgia coastal plain. The evidence of that ongoing process is found in the sedimentary rocks common in Atlanta.

If you wade in any of Atlanta's rivers, your feet are likely to emerge covered in sand and glistening slightly. The gleam comes from mica. But if you were to devote much time to panning in the Chattahoochee, there is a remote chance you might collect a few grains of the real thing — gold.

Don't forget that the expression, "There's gold in them thar hills!" originated in the North Georgia town of Dahlonega. It was used in an exhortation by a townsman trying to prevent an exodus of prospectors to California. He didn't succeed, and today only a few diehards still seek their fortunes in Dahlonega's gold mines. But between 1890 and 1933, before the Dahlonega deposits were worked out, 100,000 ounces of gold were extracted from the hills. And the Old Gainesville Belt of the Dahlonega seam runs through small sections of northwest Cobb, Cherokee, and Forsyth counties.

But before you pick up pan, pick and shovel and rush out to get rich quick, remember the caution of a report of the Department of Natural Resources: "The idea that the gold deposits of Georgia are largely undeveloped and that many rich ore bodies lie buried in the gold belt awaiting intelligent prospecting and development has no basis in fact."

You have been warned!

Stone Mountain: Not Frozen In Time

Stone Mountain Park, conceived as a monument to the South and to the heroes of the Confederacy, is much more than that: it's also Atlanta's playground.

Dominating the 3,200-acre park is the single, great, grey, granite outcrop that rises 825 feet above the surrounding plain. And commanding the attention of all are the giant figures of three Confederate heroes — Jefferson Davis, Robert E. Lee and Stonewall Jackson — carved on the mountain's sheer northern slope.

Billed as the world's largest single sculpture, the dimensions of the carving are staggering. According to the Stone Mountain Memorial Association, it occupies "a niche in the mountain the size of a city block. The figure of Lee is roughly the height of a nine-story building. His horse Traveller is about the size of five steam locomotives," and a car could easily be driven up Traveller's back, if you wished to make the attempt. Conceived in the early 1920's, the carving was not completed until 1970 because of a variety of disputes and financial problems.

Though Stone Mountain's associations hark back to the past, its pleasures are very much those of the present. There's boating and bicycling and barbecuing. There's hiking and swimming and camping and old autos and hurdy-gurdies and tennis and horse-shows and fishing.

And there are special events, like the Easter Sunrise Service and Great Easter Egg Hunt, and the Yellow Daisy Festival, and 4th of July fireworks, and live "pops" and recorded classical concerts on warm summer evenings under the benign gaze of the three generals.

The Old South meets the New . . . and warmly greets it.

159

ATLANTA'S

There are no fewer than six State Parks in the 15-county metropolitan area — seven, if you include Stone Mountain. Here we'll list only the four where over-

Park	Location	Tel./Town	Site's Special Features	Total tent & trailer campsites	With electrical hookups	With water hookups
Hard Labor Creek	2 mi. N. of Rutledge Take I-20 to Rutledge exit; head north	1-557-2863 Rutledge	fishing, golf, 3 lakes	105	105	105
High Falls	Take I-75 S. to High Falls Rd. exit Head east 1.8 miles	1-912-994-5080 1-912-994-6389 Jackson	High Falls lake, fishing, shoals, dam, mill ruins	142	142	142
Indian Springs	Take I-75 S. to McDonough/Locust Grove exit (Ga. 42) S. on Ga. 42. Park is 6 mi. SE of Jackson	1-775-7241 Indian Springs	Indian museum lake, sulphur spring	125	-	125
Red Top Mountain	Take I-75 N to Red Top Mtn/ Bethany Rd. exit	974-5182 Cartersville	Lake Alla-toona, swim-ing	275	200	200

STATE PARKS

night stays are possible. The day-use parks — Sweetwater Creek and Panola Mountain — are described in the hiking section.

										Facilities							
Comfort stations	Dump stations	Trading post	Trails	Golf	Pioneer camping area	Group camp	Swimming	Playground	Private boats allowed	Fishing boat rentals	Museum/exhibits	Boat docks	Cottages	Boat ramps	Skiing permitted	Fishing	Site acreage
4	✓	✓	✓	✓	✓	✓	Beach	4	10 hp	✓	-	✓	20	✓	-	✓	5804
5	✓	-	✓	-	✓	-	Beach	4	10 hp	✓	-	✓	-	✓	-	✓	981
5	✓	-	✓	-	✓	✓	Beach	2	10 hp	✓	✓	✓	10	✓	-	✓	510
8	✓	✓	✓	-	✓	-	Beach	2	Yes	-	-	-	18	✓	✓	✓	1950

THE RIVER
OF
FLOWERING STONES

On its winding journey from the hills of North Georgia to the Gulf of Mexico, the Chattahoochee River flows through Atlanta. It is a river that can literally be described as life-giving, not only for the wildlife in its waters and along its shores, but also for the human inhabitants of the region. For it is from this broad stream that much of Atlanta's water supply is drawn.

Archaeological remains dating back thousands of years testify to the antiquity of human associations with the river. In more recent times, it served as the boundary between the Creek and the Cherokee Indians.

The Creek legacy survives in the name, Chattahoochee. The name is translated as River of the Painted Rock by those who believe it refers to symbol messages drawn by Creek braves on a cliff overhang further downstream, and as River of Flowering Stones by those who think it derives from the moss-covered rocks fround in some parts of the river.

The Chattahoochee is among the most heavily used recreational rivers in the nation. During the 70's, as recreational use and development pressures along its shores intensified, a movement to protect the river got underway. In 1973, a tough land-use law imposing strict controls and oversight procedures for developments along the Chattahoochee was passed by the Georgia General Assembly. But the real break-through came in August 1978. That was when the U. S. Congress enacted legislation authorizing the creation of a 6,300 acre national park in 14 parcels along a 48-mile stretch of the Chattahoochee.

Under the enabling act, the National Park Service was authorized to spend $72,900,000 to acquire the necessary land along the portion of the river from Buford Dam south to the vicinity of Peachtree Creek. Some 1,000 acres already in public ownership were also turned over to the Service.

The park eventually created, to be known as the Chattahoochee River National Recreation Area (NRA), may turn out to be far smaller than the

162

6,300 acres provided for. That's because one of the first acts of the Reagan administration was to halt all acquisition of land for national parks. Still, the 3,500 acres now owned by the National Park Service offer much to be grateful for.

The Parcels

The fourteen tracts that would make up the Chattahoochee NRA — as originally planned — range in size from mere put-in points for canoes with related parking areas, to extensive wooded parcels criss-crossed with hiking trails, archaeological sites and scenic areas. Some are already relatively developed, others still in a state of nature.

When using hiking trails originating in residential areas, the National Park Service asks that you respect the rights of private property: don't trespass, block driveways, or obstruct roads.

Standing Peachtree

Standing Peachtree is the southernmost parcel in the NRA. It was the site of an Indian village used by Creek and Cherokee as a common meeting ground. Later, in 1814, a fort was built there by U. S. soldiers. The fort, at 2630 Ridgewood Road, N.W., was reconstructed as a Bicentennial project. It was also from Standing Peachtree that the first permanent ferry across the Chattahoochee plied to and fro.

The Palisades

Among the most beautiful of the park areas is The Palisades, upstream from Standing Peachtree. Here the rafter floats between high, wooded cliffs from Powers Ferry landing over mild rapids to the take-out point below U.S. 41.

For the hiker, too, the area offers several beautiful trails.

The Chattahoochee Trail leads down a forested hill to the river.

Take I-285 N to the Powers Ferry exit. Turn south, then right on Powers Ferry Road. Cross the river heading west, and turn left on Akers Mill Road — it's gravel and slippery. Park in the designated lot near the top of the hill. The trail begins at a metal gate a little further up the road.

The Overlook Trail leads to a viewing platform overlooking the Chattahoochee. When you return to the trail, follow the path to the right; it will lead you down to the river and an ancient Indian rock shelter.

Take I-285N to the Northside Drive exit. Turn south. Follow Northside Drive to Indian Trail Road and turn right. The trail begins at the end of Indian Trail Road.

Sope Creek/Powers Ferry

On the northern side of I-285, adjoining The Palisades, is the Sope Creek/

Powers Ferry park unit. The Chattahoochee in this area is much beloved of trout fishermen who, even on the coldest days of winter, can be seen waist deep and inner-tube girded, trying their luck. There are trails both along the Chattahoochee and Sope Creek.

The River Trail is a level path that follows the river past shoals and cliffs. It is popular with joggers too.

Take I-285 N to the Powers Ferry exit; turn north, then first left on Interstate North Parkway. The park entrance is just beyond the bridge.

The Sope Creek Trail will take you past the ruins of a paper mill where Confederate money was printed until General Sherman burned the mill.

Take I-285 N to the Riverside Drive exit. Turn north. Take Riverside Drive till it intersects Johnson Ferry Road, then turn left. At Paper Mill Road turn left (there is a big Atlanta Country Club Estates sign here). Follow Paper Mill Road two miles to bridge and park beyond bridge. There are trails on either side of Sope Creek.

The Pond Trail winds through woods and around a pond.

Follow Sope Creek instructions but proceed further up Paper Mill Road after you have crossed the bridge. Park near a brown metal gate, and walk back about 300 yards. The trail is a dirt track to your left.

Morgan Falls

The Johnson Ferry site is no more than a raft put-in point, and there's another at Morgan Falls off Roswell Road.

But Morgan Falls also offers hiking trails on the northern side of the river, and, above the old hydroelectric dam that for many years supplied power to Sandy Springs, can be seen Civil War gun emplacements.

The Morgan Falls Trails are unmarked, but lead down to the river. Use of the trail map available from the National Park Service (tel.: 952-6009) is advised.

Take Ga. 400 north of I-285 to the Northridge Road exit. Turn west on Northridge, then right on Roswell. At Azalea Drive, just beyond the bridge over the Chattahoochee, turn left. Continue on Azalea until it deadends into Willeo and take the left fork. Continue on Willeo until it becomes Lower Roswell Road. The entrance into Morgan Falls West is opposite Willow Point subdivision on Lower Roswell.

Big Creek and Island Ford

Upstream from Morgan Falls, the Big Creek and Island Ford tracts offer both natural beauty and a good wildlife and botanical habitat. Along the Big Creek itself are the ruins of the textile mill built by Roswell King in 1839. The mill was destroyed by Sherman during the Civil War because it supplied the Confederate army with uniforms. It was later rebuilt, then partially gutted by fire in 1926, but continued to operate until 1975, when its owners closed it down for the last time.

The Big Creek Trail will take you along Big Creek and, with some luck, to the ruins of the Ivy Woolen Mill. Use of a Park Service trail map is helpful, but not essential.

164

The Chattahoochee at Jones Bridge

Take Ga. 400 north of I-285 to the Northridge Road exit. Go west on Northridge, then right on Roswell Road. At Oxbo Drive, just beyond Roswell Square, turn right, then right again on Grimes Bridge Road. Trails lead off Grimes Bridge Road at three points, the most obvious being at a metal gate to your right.

The Island Ford Trail leads down a hill to the Chattahoochee; smooth rocks in the river encourage sunbathing. The trail continues for 2½ miles along the river; it was built by Eagle Scouts and leads to the old Georgia Baptist Assembly.

Follow Big Creek directions to Roswell Road. Turn right on Roswell, then right on Roberts Drive (just before the river). Follow Roberts Drive until you reach an upright marker for Island Ferry Road opposite the Dunwoody Place condominiums. Turn left at the marker and park in the gravel lot. When you have hiked to the bottom of the hill, cross a small stream and take the trail to the left to reach the river.

Jones Bridge

The Holcomb Bridge site is still totally undeveloped. But at the Jones Bridge Park upstream is one of the most scenic spots on the river, with picnic facilities, excellent fishing, and the ruins of the old bridge still straddling part of the Chattahoochee.

Take I-285 N to Peachtree Industrial Boulevard exit (Ga. 141). North on Peachtree Industrial. Left on Jones Bridge Road.

Medlock Bridge

The bridge spanning the stream at the Medlock Bridge site is also in disrepair. This small tract serves mainly as a canoe put-in point, but it also offers a hiking trail.

Follow Jones Bridge directions, but continue on Ga. 141, which becomes Medlock Bridge Road, until it passes over the Chattahoochee.

Bowman's Island

The projected Abbott's Bridge, Suwanee Creek and Settles' Bridge parks are still undeveloped, but Bowman's Island, the last of the 14 parcels, offers excellent trout fishing, and there is a State Trout Hatchery on the Chattahoochee's northern shore. The site also serves as a put-in point, and offers picnic facilities.

Take Ga. 400 to Ga. 20 exit. Right on Ga. 20, then left on Buford Dam Road (or take I-85 to the Buford exit, then Ga. 20).

Other Parks on the Chattahoochee

Upstream from Morgan Falls, and outside the NRA itself, is the Chattahoochee Nature Center. A private, non-profit corporation, the Center's primary purpose is educational, but it also provides a boardwalk hiking trail. On your way to the Center, you'll pass the **Chattahoochee River Park**. This park is operated by Fulton County, and offers boating, fishing, a boardwalk trail, and a children's playground. The reeded marshes through which the Chattahoochee meanders here are rich in bird and other animal life.

Follow Morgan Falls directions most of the way. The Chattahoochee River Park is on Azalea Drive, the Nature Center on Willeo Road's left fork.

Horticulturists Ahoy!

One of the great pleasures of the outdoors life is that of seeing live green things poking out of the earth as the result of one's own efforts in planning and cultivating a garden. And it is an activity which may bring one into a community of like-minded souls. In Atlanta, garden clubs bloom in many neighborhoods, and club projects often include the florification of barren public spaces.

The fledgling Atlanta Botanical Garden (tel.: 876-5858) in Piedmont Park is an attempt to create a true public garden in a city which sorely lacks one. Two and a half of the five cultivated acres that form part of the Garden are demonstration gardens, where experts offer instruction on topics of interest to amateur gardeners. The remaining acres offer a rose garden, a Japanese garden, and herb and vegetable gardens. Adjacent to these, the city maintains a greenhouse with tropical plants.

There is also a special place for ardent horticulturists: the Cherokee Garden Library at the Atlanta Historical Society, 3101 Andrews Drive, N.W. Here is housed a collection of rare and current books, magazines, and pamphlets related to all aspects of gardening.

Callaway Gardens, some 90 miles south of Atlanta, are worth seeing at almost any time of the year, but magnificent in spring when more than 600 varieties of azalea are in bloom.

In spring, also, one may glimpse some of Atlanta's secret gardens, put on display by their owners to benefit the Atlanta Music Club as part of the annual Dogwood Festival.

BEST FOOT FORWARD
Hiking in Atlanta

The English call it Shanks's pony: the use of one's own legs as a means of transportation. Shanks's pony has many advantages over other modes of travel. It is cheap, healthful, and invigorating; and, in Atlanta, it will lead you over much scenic terrain, through wooded hills, and along broad streams.

This section introduces readers to the nicest of the many hiking trails in and around the Atlanta area. None of the hikes described here is beyond the capacity of the average walker, and some, designated with a *, are more in the nature of strolls. Most can be completed within an hour or two. Hikes within the Chattahoochee National Recreation Area are described in "The River of Flowering Stones" section.

To make it easier for the reader to get his bearings, Atlanta's hiking areas have been listed according to their geographical location. I-20 is taken as the dividing line between north and south, and U.S. 19 as the boundary between east and west.

Northeast

Alexander Park
East Wesley Road, N.E.
Atlanta

This small (11-acre) wooded park in the heart of Garden Hills offers a pleasant trail through the woods.

Elwyn Jones Wildlife Sanctuary
Holly Lane
DeKalb

168

Another oasis in a built-up area, this 7-acre tract is managed by the Atlanta Audubon Society. It contains several nature trails — but beware the poison ivy which infests the area.

Take I-85 to the North Druid Hills exit; head east on North Druid Hills Road. Holly Lane is to your right just beyond Briarcliff High School. Park in Holly Lane, walk up Gatchell School drive to dirt road leading into sanctuary.

Fernbank Forest
156 Heaton Park Drive, N.E.
DeKalb

This 65-acre natural area is threaded by paved pathways. By visiting the adjacent Exhibition Hall with its scientific displays, you can combine a hike with a little learning. Off Ponce de Leon Avenue.
Open: Sun.-Fri., 2-5 pm; Sat., 10 am - 5 pm.

Providence Road Park
13313   Providence Road
Alpharetta

This park offers three short nature trails as well as a variety of courses in outdoor skills such as backpacking, camping, fishing, and environmental studies. For information, telephone 475-9313.

Stone Mountain Park
off U.S. 78
DeKalb

Stone Mountain has a couple of not very interesting nature trails. They're No. 47 on the map you'll receive as you enter the Park.
For the more robust, the steep hike up the mountain is invigorating, and gives you a pleasant feeling of superiority over the indolent who take the cable-car. Start this walk from "The War in Georgia" parking lot. There is a charge to enter the park.

Southeast

Arabia Mountain Park
3850 Klondike Road
Lithonia

More accurately a hill, Arabia Mountain is composed of the Lithonia Gneiss unique to Atlanta. It's an easy walk to the top. The park is not developed,

THE INSIDER'S ATLANTA

and no security is provided.
Take I-20 E to the Lithonia/Evans Mill Road exit. South on Evans Mill Road, left on Woodrow Drive, right on Klondike Road.

Panola Mountain State Park
2600 Highway 155
Stockbridge
Tel.: 474-2914

Panola is a little Stone Mountain. It is managed by the Georgia Department of Natural Resources as an interpretive center. Special programs are held here throughout the year.

Panola offers two types of trail: self-guided strolls,* each about ¾ mile long, through rocky and wooded areas; and two or three-hour guided hikes to the top of the mountain and along the lake. The longer hikes are conducted on Thursdays, Saturdays and Sundays (call for exact times), and they're guided to prevent people from disturbing delicate ecosystems. You'll observe how natural forces weather rock, and how succession takes place from simple organisms clinging to patches of soil to more complex forms.
Take I-285 E to Flat Shoals Road (Ga. 155) exit. South on Ga. 155. (Flat Shoals Road deadends into Snapfinger Road; right on Snapfinger, which becomes Ga. 155). Or take I-20 E to Wesley Chapel Road/Snapfinger Road exit. Right on Wesley Chapel. Left at first traffic light (Snapfinger Road). Carry on on Snapfinger approximately 10 miles. Park is on left.

Southwest

Outdoor Activity Center
1442 Richland Road, S.W.
Atlanta
Tel.: 752-5385

This is one of those small natural oases that tend to keep surprising you in the very heart of the city. The Outdoor Activity Center's Bush Mountain Trail is one of only a handful of urban trails designated a National Recreation Trail.

The land which the Center occupies is owned by the City of Atlanta, but the Center is a non-profit educational corporation. Large groups should make prior arrangements to visit. For a modest charge, the services of a trained naturalist are also available. The Center also has a small, wild animal rehabilitation center and exhibit room.
To reach the trail, take I-20 W to the Lee Street/West End exit. Left on Lee. Go 1 mile to Donnelly Avenue, right on Donnelly, left on Oakland Road, then right on Richland. (You're advised to take a companion on the hike.) To reach the Center, continue on Oakland to a flashing yellow light; turn left on Bridges.

Open: M-F., 8:30 am - 4:30 pm; Sat., 12 - 3 pm.

*Sandtown Park
5320 Campbellton Road
Atlanta
Tel.: 344-3209

Two trails, each about ½ mile long, wind through the woods. Call the day before to make arrangements. Open: M.-Sat., 11 am - 6 pm.

Sweetwater Creek State Park
Mt. Vernon Road
Lithia Springs
Tel.: 944-1700

Sweetwater Creek rises in Paulding County. As it flows through Douglas County on its way to join the Chattahoochee, it bubbles between steep banks and around rock shoals to create one of the most beautiful areas in the metropolitan region.

Among the Park's chief attractions are ruins. The ruins are those of the New Manchester Manufacturing Company's textile mill, which was in operation from 1849 to 1864. In that fateful year, the mill, like so many others, was razed by Sherman's troops because of its role in supplying the Confederate army, and its employees were shipped north to Kentucky and Indiana. It was never rebuilt.

The park offers the hiker two trails: the East Ridge trail, to reach which you must cross the creek by bridge, takes you down to a small waterfall and scenic overlook. The Factory Ruins trail takes you past the mill ruins and along the creek's western bank.

For those interested in Sweetwater Creek's fascinating geology, a geologic guide to the Park is available from the Georgia Department of Natural Resources.

From Atlanta, take I-20 W to the Lee Road/Lithia Springs exit. Turn right on Lee Road, right on Sweetwater Road (which becomes Mt. Vernon). The park entrance is to your left just beyond the George Sparks Reservoir.

W. H. Reynolds Nature Preserve
Reynolds Road.
Morrow

This beautiful 120-acre wooded area offers a network of hiking trails, four ponds — the largest of which can be fished — and running trails of varying lengths.

Take I-75 S to the Morrow exit. Turn left (north) onto Jonesboro Road (Ga. 54). At third traffic light, turn left onto Reynolds Road. The Preserve is on your left.

Note: From the Preserve, you can make a pleasant excursion to the historic Rex Mill on Rex Road. Turn right out of the Preserve's parking lot, then first left on Huie Road. Continue on Huie (beyond Ga. 54 it becomes Harper Drive) until it deadends into Rex Road. Right on Rex; after a few miles the little red mill will appear on your left. For 130 years, until it ceased operation in 1963, it fulfilled its original function.

Northwest

Etowah Trail
off Shoal Creek Road
Canton
Cherokee County

This 2½ mile trail was created by boy scouts as a Bicentennial project. You'll pass Signature Rock, with inscriptions chiselled on it, and the old Canton-Sutallee Roadway, which runs parallel to the Etowah River.

Take I-75 N to the Ga. 5 exit. Head north on Ga. 5. Just beyond Canton, turn left on Ga. 140, then left again on Shoal Creek Road. At a fork in the road about 1.2 miles further on, veer left. Veer left again at a second fork. A sign marking the trail and gravel parking area are on the left.

Kennesaw Mountain National Battlefield Park
Old U.S. 41, N.W.
Marietta

The red hills of this part of Georgia were soaked with the red blood of Confederate and Yankee soldiers in one of the grimmest battles of the Civil War. It was a battle in which 150,000 men were engaged for 23 grueling, often rain-drenched days. The 40,000 Confederates, securely entrenched on Kennesaw's steep slopes, inflicted terrible losses on Sherman's assault forces. Only when rank upon rank had fallen, did Sherman finally give the order to withdraw.

The hiker can still see the trenches behind which the forces of the South lay hidden, pouring leaden fire on the enemy. Cannon on Kennesaw's summit are another memorial to the Confederates' brief moment of glory. In the Park's Visitors' Center relics are displayed.

The peace of the past 116 years has done much to heal Kennesaw's scars. Twelve miles of wooded trails now make the battlefield a boon for hikers. Maps showing hiking trails are available from the Visitors' Center.

Take I-75N to the Kennesaw Park exit, and follow the signs.

Swan Woods Trail
Swan House
3130 Slaton Drive, NW
Atlanta

Sweetwater Creek

A pleasant stroll through the carefully-kept grounds of Swan House will strain nobody's energies.
Off West Paces Ferry Road near Sears.
Open: Tu. - Sat., 10:30 am - 5 pm; Sun., 1:30 - 5 pm

Wildwood Park
corner of South Cobb Drive and Barclay Circle
Marietta

This 28-acre park created from Federal surplus land offers 2½ miles of hiking and nature trails as well as a 1/10 mile nature trail. In addition, a variety of outdoors programs are offered by the Marietta Parks and Recreation Department (tel.: 492-4211). These include nature walks, orienteering courses that teach youngsters 12 years and up how to read a topographical map, and challenge-adventure courses for ages six and up. Several adult programs are also offered.

Conservationists

Here is a list of the major conservation and outdoors-oriented groups in the Atlanta area.

Organization	Telephone
Atlanta Audubon Society 440 Nelson Ferry Rd. Decatur	373-8474
The Georgia Conservancy 3110 Maple Dr., N.E., Suite 407	262-1967
The Georgia Heritage Trust Program Georgia Department of Natural Resources 270 Washington St., S.W.	
The Sierra Club, Atlanta Group 673 Crespan Court Lawrenceville	972-3557

MESSING ABOUT
IN BOATS

Atlanta, though it lacks the sea, brims over with lakes, not one natural. For the many blessings they have conferred on them, boat dealers can thank the U.S. Army Corps of Engineers and other human beavers with a penchant for building dams.

Lake Lanier (tel.: 945-6701) is perhaps Atlanta's most popular summer resort. Here pontoons, houseboats, sailboats, and fishing boats are available for hire; so are fishing pro's to guide you to the best fishing holes. Lake Lanier's other attractions include swimming, trout fishing, golfing, waterskiing, stables and horse trails, and a choice of a hotel, cottages, or campsites to stay in.

Other large bodies of water in the metro area are Lake Allatoona and Lake Jackson, which borders Butts and Newton Counties in the southeast. In these lakes, you can fish, boat, waterski, or swim.

Row, Row Your Boat. . .

For more than 150 years, the art of competitive rowing has been associated with the great universities of Oxford and Cambridge, and with their annual boat race on the River Thames. Now a group of enthusiasts is attempting to stimulate interest in the sport in Atlanta.

The Atlanta Rowing Club, which boasts members from many countries, sponsors sculling and sweep rowing. It has its own clubhouse on the Chattahoochee River, near the intersection of Roswell Road and Azalea Drive. Members generally meet on Saturday and Sunday mornings, and beginners' clinics are also offered. For information, contact Mr. Clay Bristow (tel.: 873-2693).

Gently Down the Stream...

For drifters, nothing more than an inflated inner tube or a raft is necessary. The mighty Chattahoochee will carry you along. Take-out point is the bridge that carries U.S. 41 over the river. But you can launch your vessel at a number of points upstream, including Bowman's Island, Medlock Bridge (both of which are probably too distant for a day's outing), Morgan Falls, Johnsons Ferry, and Powers Ferry Landing.

A raft-rental concession has been granted to a company called the Chattahoochee Outdoor Center (tel.: 394-6622) at the U.S. 41, Powers Island, and Johnsons Ferry sites. The company also offers a shuttle-bus service between these locations; it is scheduled to run every 20 minutes on weekends, and every 30 minutes on week days, from May 1 through Labor Day.

A raft rental concession is also operated by the Sandy Springs Jaycees (tel.: 256-0168) at the Powers Ferry Landing site owned by Fulton County. The service operates from 10 am - 5 pm on Mondays, Wednesdays, Thursdays, and Fridays from March through April, and every day from May through September.

It's advisable to reserve a raft in advance if you're planning on a Saturday or Sunday outing.

Paddle Your Own Canoe

If you'd rather paddle your own canoe, rent one at Stone Mountain, and enjoy the peace of the lake with its stately paddle-steamer churning by.

Canoes can also be rented on an hourly, half-day or daily basis from Chattahoochee Canoe Rental, Inc. (tel.: 998-7778), which operates a concession at Fulton County's Chattahoochee River Park near Roswell (directions on page 167.) Instruction is also offered.

Those who prefer the thrill of whitewater can find it, too. There is good canoeing to be had on the Chattahoochee and its tributaries, as well as some other streams. Canoes can be rented from many sporting-goods stores.

The Georgia Canoeing Association organizes canoeing expeditions every weekend during 10 months of the year. For a $10 annual subscription, members receive copies of the association's newsletter listing planned excursions and a guidebook describing Georgia's whitewater rivers. The association also offers training clinics for beginners, and sponsors the Southeastern U.S. Whitewater Championships each June on North Carolina's Nantahala River. The association's address is P. O. Box 7023, Atlanta, Ga. 30357.

THE HUNTIN', SHOOTIN', FISHIN' SET

D'ye ken John Peel when he's far far away
With his hounds and his horn in the morning?...
For Peel's view-hollo would waken the dead
Or a fox from his lair in the morning.

Twice a week, from October through March, the 200 members of the **Shakerag Hunt Club** follow the hounds up the hills and down the dales of Shakerag, in northeast Fulton, on the scent of a hapless fox.

As befits an ancient sport, the club's tradition is stylish. Huntsmen wear formal dress in the club colors — Confederate gray — except for those hunters of excellence who have earned the right to wear pink coats, and Saturday hunts culminate in an elegant breakfast. The Shakerag hounds are said to be one of the finest packs in Georgia.

Membership in the Shakerag Club is by invitation only, and you must be proposed by a member. But anyone can attend the annual **Atlanta Hunt Meet and Steeplechase** which coincidentally marks the end of the hunting year. Elegant picnics are the rule at this event, which is held in the second week of April on a private farm near Cumming, Georgia. There is an admission charge.
Take I-285 North to I-400 North. Take the Ga. 20 exit (left off I-400) until it dead-ends into Ga. 19, left again on Ga. 19, then left on Ga. 141. Steeplechase exit is on right off 141.

Good Shooting

Your true Georgian will hunt most anything, even squirrels if nothing better offers. So it's not surprising that hunting territory has been set aside in the metro area, or that marksmen can keep their eye in at shooting ranges in the off-season.

Hunting licenses are required, and a special stamp is needed to hunt in Wildlife Management Areas. There are also specific quotas and hunting seasons applicable to different species of game and management areas.

If you'd like to improve your skill with a gun and reduce the chance of accident, enroll in one of the Department of Natural Resources' brief hunter education certification courses. For more information, contact the Department's Education Section, 714 Trinity-Washington Building, Atlanta, Georgia 30334.

Shooting Ranges	Telephone	Hours
DeKalb Firing Range 3905 North Goddard Road Lithonia	482-8965	W-Sat., 10 am - 6 pm Sun., 1 - 6 pm
Wolf Creek Trap and Skeet Range 3070 Merk Road, SW Fulton County	346-1545	M - Th., 4:30 - 10 pm Sat. & Sun., 10 am - 6 pm

Game Hunting

Allatoona Management Area Lake Allatoona Bartow & Cherokee Counties	656-3530	
Redbone Farm Hunting Preserve Community Home Road Barnesville, Ga. 30204	1-358-1658	

The Compleat Angler

"No life, my honest scholar, no life so happy and so pleasant as the life of a well-governed angler."

So spake Izaak Walton back in 1653.

The true delights of "this pleasant curiosity of Fish and Fishing" are known only to the dedicated angler. And he can find them aplenty in the bountiful waters of Atlanta's lakes and rivers.

Perhaps the most remarkable feature of fishing in Atlanta is that it is possible to catch trout in sparkling streams in the very heart of the urban area. The state stocks some 150,000 trout in the Chattahoochee each year. Above Morgan Falls, rainbow and brook trout are most common; below, brown trout.

Other plentiful species are yellow perch and sunfish. Sweetwater Creek is also rich in trout.

Lakes Lanier, Allatoona and Jackson all offer good sport for the fisherman. For a dollar or two, he can also spend a pleasant day fishing in one of the myriad private lakes scattered all over the metro area or in dams like the George C. Sparks Reservoir in Douglas County.

All fishermen over the age of 16 are required to have a current fishing license in their possession while fishing in fresh water, and a Trout Stamp is necessary for anglers who favor trout. There are also limits on the number of fish you may catch. For more information, consult the Department of Natural Resources' Information office at 270 Washington Street, SW, Atlanta, Georgia 30334.

XI

GOOD SPORT!

Running the Peachtree

TEAMED UP—
AND STEAMED UP

In sports, as with many things, it's true that nothing succeeds like success. And after years of unfulfilled performances by local teams, the promise of success for Atlanta's professional sportsmen still has the power to rouse the Atlanta public from a kind of forgiving tolerance to a partisan peak.

The major leagues were first attracted to Atlanta in the 1960's by the construction of a modern stadium to replace homely Ponce Park, and by the eager solicitations of the city fathers. The Milwaukee Braves baseball team changed hats and became the Atlanta Braves. Soon Atlanta acquired a pro football team, the Atlanta Falcons, who were followed in due course by the Atlanta Hawks basketball team.

The Braves got off to a good start. In particular, there was the fabled occasion when Hank Aaron hit his 715th home run. Aaron ranks right up there with Coke and "Gone With the Wind" as a genuine Atlanta legend.

By the late 1970's, though, the Braves' standing had declined, reaching its low point one season with a string of losses nearly equaling the league record. Since then, the Braves have been rebuilding. They're still not the Yankees, but their fans have taken fresh heart — and went wild when the Braves opened the 1982 season with a record-breaking 13-0 winning streak.

Supporters of the Falcons, after a long wait, finally had their reward in 1981 when the team, reconstituted with many young players, made it to the Superbowl playoffs, eventually going down to a narrow and honorable defeat by the Dallas Cowboys.

In basketball, the Hawks are ranked among the top teams, with some of the best players in the NBA.

"Third time lucky" appears to be the watchword for professional soccer in the city. Two tribes of Chiefs have risen and died in Atlanta; yet their last rites were barely over before it was announced that a new team would take their place. Discarding the shadow of the past, the new team enters the future with a new name, the Georgia Generals, and in a new arena, the 15,000 seat DeKalb Memorial Stadium near Memorial Drive.

THE INSIDER'S ATLANTA

A College Collage

The big names in college sports are Georgia Tech and the University of Georgia, though Morris Brown College also has a strong football team.

The Tech football team is the Yellow Jackets. It's named after a nasty, waspish insect that carries a sting in its tail. In the past, the Jackets were associated with a string of well-known coaches. The first was John Heisman, after whom the Heisman Trophy is named. He was followed by Bill Alexander and Bobby Dodd. The Jackets were reputedly the first team to go to all four Bowls: Rose, Orange, Sugar, and Cotton.

The University of Georgia's Georgia Bulldogs are based in Athens, but so many Georgia alumni live in Atlanta that the Bulldogs are as good as a home team. So there was jubilation all around, and a heroes' welcome, when the Bulldogs, coached by Vince Dooley, pulled off the big one — the conquest of Notre Dame, and victory in the 1981 Sugar Bowl.

One of the highlights of the college football season is the Yellow Jackets' annual clash with the Bulldogs. It's a tradition that began in 1905, and, as *Atlanta Journal* columnist Furman Bisher wrote in one of his columns, "From Whigham to Hiawassee, it was a matter of gravity and passion."

A matter of much less passion is the annual Peach Bowl held in Atlanta in January. The Peach nearly rotted into oblivion in 1978 because fans could not be persuaded to bite. But it recovered its bloom and network coverage in 1979. The Bowl is worth supporting, even if you don't care who wins, because proceeds go to the Georgia Lighthouse for the Blind.

Ticketing

Here's how to order your tickets for professional sports events. For Georgia Tech games, call 894-5447.

Team	Season	Arena	Telephone
Braves	April - Sept.	Stadium	577-9100
Falcons	Fall	Stadium	325-2667
Georgia Generals	Summer	DeKalb Memorial Stadium	491-7555
Hawks	Oct. - April	Omni	577-9600

Tickets for these events are also available from all SEATS outlets (681-2100).

JOGGING
ALONG

The dedicated runner, it is said, obtains spiritual peace through jogging. The non-athletic among us may regard this activity simply as a needless mortification of the flesh.

Whether you're running for the first reason or because you have an excessive amount of flesh in urgent need of mortification, Atlanta offers plenty of opportunity to achieve your goal.

The competitive runner in Atlanta need never sit still. The Atlanta Track Club (tel.: 231-9064) organizes some 50 road races a year, including the mammoth Peachtree Road Race. Stamina and a love of humanity at close quarters are all you need to compete in this, Atlanta's premier amateur athletic event. And if pounding the tarmac is your bag, it's as good a way to celebrate the Fourth of July as any.

Runners come from all over the country to take part in this race. In fact, the number who may participate has now been limited to 25,000. Most runners who assemble at the starting point at Lenox Square complete the 6.2 mile course one way or another. The real triumph comes in reaching the finishing line in Piedmont Park in less than 55 minutes, and winning a T-shirt to prove it. (As a little extra incentive, a purse totalling $25,000 was recently added to the race.) A separate competition for wheelchair athletes along the same course begins an hour before the main race.

Some public schools allow runners to use their tracks after school hours and on weekends. Check with the principal of the school in your neighborhood to make sure.

Here, by county, are some outdoor tracks and trails you may want to try:

THE INSIDER'S ATLANTA

Grady Stadium
cnr. 8th Street and Charles Allen Drive
(tel.: 872-3808)

Use is permitted in daylight hours after school and on weekends when not in school use.

Peyton Forest Park
Peyton Road, S. W.

This park offers a ¾ mile track around the baseball field.

Piedmont Park
Piedmont Road, N. E.

Joggers use the path around the lake as a convenient track.

Clayton County

W. H. Reynolds Nature Preserve
Reynolds Road
Morrow

Several miles of running trails of various lengths. Off Jonesboro Road (Ga. 54).

Cobb County

Cobb County Civic Center
cnr. Fairground and Clay Streets.

There is a jogging track around the complex.

Fuller's Park Jogging Trail
Robinson Road
Marietta

This long-distance track has earned statewide acclaim.

Hickory Hills Park
cnr. Hickory Dr. and Chestnut Hill Road
Marietta

Laurel Park
151 Manning Road
Marietta

Wildwood Park
cnr. South Cobb Drive and Barclay Circle
Marietta

The three parks listed above all offer jogging tracks, some equipped with fitness stations.

DeKalb County

DeKalb Community College
555 N. Indian Creek Drive
Clarkston

Open air track with marked stops for fitness exercises at 1, 1½ and 2½-mile intervals. Park behind stadium.

Tucker Park
4259 N. Ball Park Drive
Tucker

Douglas County

Hunter Park
975 Pinecrest Drive
Douglasville

A
SPORTS
OMNIBUS

The sportsman in Atlanta can polo with the polite and ski with the skilled. Or he can bowl with the beerbellies and wrestle with the rough.

He can join a private club — whether an exclusive and high-priced country club or one of Atlanta's many commercial athletic and fitness centers — or he can fulfill his sporting urges without spending a cent. Most county and city governments provide excellent athletic facilities free, including free tennis courts, gyms, running tracks, ball fields, and softball courts.

In addition, the YMCA's of Atlanta offer gym, swimming, softball, and racquetball facilities for their male and female members. The Downtown Y, 145 Luckie Street, enables office workers to keep in shape during lunch hours and after work. The **Atlanta Jewish Community Centers**, 1745 Peachtree Road, NE and 5342 Tilly Mill Road, Doraville, also offer many sport and athletic amenities to members at reasonable rates; membership is open to all, regardless of religion.

To be exhaustive is obviously not possible in a book of this scope. Here we'll simply list specialized, mostly public facilities by county, and point you to athletic associations which can provide detailed information on specific sports. To find out about other public amenities in your neighborhood, including children's leagues, call your local Parks and Recreation Department.

You'll find specialized private athletic clubs and sports facilities listed in the Yellow Pages of the telephone directory under Athletic Organizations, Clubs, Gymnasiums, Gymnastics Instruction, and the name of the relevant sport.

Daisy, Daisy!

Atlanta with its hilly terrain is hardly ideal territory for the lazy cyclist.

But for those who love bicycling, there's plenty of action.

There's one officially designated bike route in the City of Atlanta; it winds through Piedmont Park and the Virginia-Highland neighborhood for 13½ miles, but bicycles have no separate right of way. A map of this route can be obtained from the City's Bureau of Traffic Engineering, 1003 City Hall, 68 Mitchell Street, SW, Atlanta, Georgia 30303. DeKalb County also maintains a bike route which runs roughly parallel to Ponce de Leon Avenue from Avondale Estates to Stone Mountain Park. For information, contact the DeKalb County Department of Recreation, Parks and Cultural Affairs, Courthouse Square, Decatur, Georgia 30030.

The **Southern Bicycle League** (tel.: 325-1925) organizes as many as 40 rides a month during the summer, and about half that number during the winter. Rides start from different points and will take you to many parts of the metro area.

If you're interested in venturing farther afield, a booklet called *Georgia Bikeways*, put out by the Georgia Department of Industry and Trade, contains maps and route information about 11 bike trails in various parts of the state.

Foiled Again

The fine art of fencing flourishes in Atlanta. The city also hosts the annual Atlanta Open in October, which attracts swordsmen from all over the country. For information, contact the Atlanta Fencers' Club (tel.: 892-0307), 15 5th Street, N. W., Atlanta.

Down the Fairway

In addition to the many privately-owned golf courses in Atlanta — some open to the public, some only to members — the City of Atlanta and DeKalb County maintain good public golf courses.

City/County	Golf Course	Telephone
Atlanta	Adams Park Golf Course 2300 Wilson Dr., S.W.	753-6158
	Bobby Jones Golf Course 384 Woodward Way, N.W. (cnr. Northside Dr.)	355-9049
	Browns Mill Golf Course 480 Cleveland Ave., S.E.	361-9959

	Candler Park Golf Course (9 hole) 585 Candler Park Dr., N.E.	373-9265
	North Fulton Golf Course 216 W. Wieuca Rd., N.E.	255-0723
DeKalb	Mystery Valley Golf Course 6094 Shadow Rock Dr. Lithonia	469-6913
	Sugar Creek Golf Course 2706 Bouldercrest Rd. Atlanta	241-7671
	Golfmore Driving Range 3500 North Decatur Rd. Decatur	292-9149

Horseriding

Riding arenas and/or trails have been created in Chastain Park, Atlanta (tel.: 255-9606), and Wills Park, Alpharetta (tel.: 475-3470). In addition, scores of private stables and riding schools, listed in the Yellow Pages, offer facilities for those of equestrian tastes.

Several organizations sponsor shows. Among the largest are:

Association	Telephone
Georgia Western Horse Show Association Route 1 Brooks, Ga. 30205.	1-599-8045

The Association sanctions horse-shows of local saddle clubs in the halter, English, performance, and pleasure classes of all breeds.

Georgia Quarterhorse Association Route 2, Box 535, Loganville, Ga. 30249.	466-8517

A fuller list of horseriding organizations is available from the Georgia

The Great Atlanta Balloon Race, Piedmont Park

Department of Agriculture.

Students in school systems that participate in county 4-H programs receive manuals on horse care. 4-H Clubs also sponsor shows from time to time.

High-school students who want to learn the ropes of rodeo can do so under skilled supervision. For information, contact:

Georgia High School Rodeo Association   482-2186
6522 Rock Springs Road
Lithonia,
Ga. 30058.

Polo

The headquarters of the Atlanta Polo Club are on Johnson Ferry Road where it crosses the Chattahoochee River in Cobb County. Games are played Sundays at 3:30 pm from May through October.

Rugger

If you think American football is rough, British rugby could make you think again. You'll learn some new terms, like scrum, line-out, and try. Here's a list of local clubs.

Club	Information
Atlanta Old White Rugby Club	522-0856 / 355-3460
Atlanta Renegades Rugby Club	233-5711 / 634-4098
Atlanta Rugby Football Club	366-5940 (Alex McCracken)
High Country Rugby Football Club	977-8302 (Andrew Kasper)

Women's Rugger

Atlanta Women's Rugby Football Club	233-6551 / 656-5963 (Paula Rafferty)

Downhill Racing

For information about Georgia and Southeastern ski resorts with real snow, contact the Atlanta Ski Club (tel.: 892-1286).

GOOD SPORT!

Soccer: Getting a Kick Out of Life

Some 15,000 kids, as well as thousands of adults in the metro area play soccer, mainly on public fields. There are girls' leagues too. To find out how to join a team and participate in coach and referee-training programs, contact the Georgia State Soccer Association (tel.: 452-0505). Their Soccer Newsline (tel.: 452-0511) will give you up-to-date information on forthcoming games for all age groups.

In The Swim

Many counties and cities operate public swimming pools. Contact the Parks and Recreation Department in your area to find the one nearest you. A number of YMCA's have indoor pools, as does the Atlanta Jewish Community Center. Also check with your neighborhood group; some have built pools that local residents can use on becoming members.

Don't forget the sandy white beach at Stone Mountain; it's open in summer. Farther afield, the beaches of Lakes Lanier and Allatoona lure swimmers too.

Need to brush up on your technique? Many YMCA's offer instruction for beginners as young as six months, and classes are also offered by the Red Cross (tel.: 881-9800).

Anyone for Tennis?

Most counties and cities in the metro area maintain excellent free all-weather tennis courts in neighborhood parks. Some also operate specialized Tennis Centers. There is usually a modest charge for use of courts at these Centers, but, to compensate, most also offer a clubhouse, showers, lockers, a stadium for tournament matches, a base for a local tennis association, and a tennis professional as instructor.

County/City	Tennis Center	Telephone
Atlanta	Bitsy Grant Tennis Center 2125 Northside Drive, N.W.	351-2774
	Chastain Tennis Center 4835 Powers Ferry Rd., N.W. (cnr. W. Wieuca Rd.)	255-9798
	Piedmont Tennis Center 10th Street, N.E.	872-1507

193

	Washington Park Tennis Center 1125 Lena St., N.W.	523-1169
Cobb	Fair Oaks Tennis Center Brandon Drive Marietta	424-0204
	Kennworth Park Tennis Center South Main St. (Rt. 293) Acworth	974-9515
	Sweetwater Park Tennis Center Clay Road Austell	941-9545
	Terrell Mill Tennis Center Terrell Mill Road Marietta	952-6076
DeKalb	Blackburn Tennis Center 3501 Ashford Dunwoody Rd. Chamblee	451-1061
	DeKalb Tennis Center 1400 McConnell Dr. Decatur	325-2520
Fulton	North Fulton Tennis Center 500 Abernathy Road Sandy Springs	256-1588
	South Fulton Tennis Center 5645 Mason Rd. College Park	964-1388

WHEELS

No, Atlanta's highways are not the only racetracks in the region. Of course, you have to travel a bit further to reach the others, but think what fun you can have getting there!

Local legend has it that stock-car racing originated in Georgia in the '30s. Moonshining was at its peak, and whiskey runners took pride in pitting their cars, specially modified to outrun the police, against each other. It began as friendly competition, and soon developed into a sport that flourished on tracks near Jonesboro and at the old Lakewood Speedway.

Though Atlanta is no longer the center of the stock-car racing world it is still the scene of major competitions like the Coca-Cola 500 and the *Atlanta Journal* 500. And the opportunities for the amateur to get his piece dialed in and race, hopefully without waking up Lee Roy, are good.

Here's a brief guide to Atlanta's racetracks.

Facility	Classes	Open	Telephone
Atlanta International Dragway, Inc. Ridgeway Road Commerce	Drag	Weekends, March-Oct.	1-335-2301

Take I-85 N to Commerce exit and follow signs.

Road Atlanta Off Highway 53 Braselton	GT Roadracing	Daily, throughout year	881-8233

195

THE INSIDER'S ATLANTA

Annual highlights at this track are the Champion Sparkplug Roadracing Classic in mid or late October, attended by amateurs from all over the U.S., and the Camel GT competition, a professional event held twice a year in April and September. Driver-training instruction is offered. Motorcycle and go-kart clubs may also rent the track.

Take I-85 N to Braselton exit (Highway 53), south on 53, carry on 5 miles to Road Atlanta exit on left.

Atlanta International Raceway, Inc. S. Expressway Hampton	Stockcar, motocross, tractor-pull Bobtail-truck	Throughout year, call for race-dates	946-4211

Some items on this list may be unfamiliar. In tractor-pull competition, the special tractor that pulls a weight furthest wins. Bobtail-truck races involve the front-sections of 18 wheelers. Annual highlights include the International Race of Champions held in March, and the Coca-Cola 500 and *Atlanta Journal* 500 Grand National stock car races, held respectively in March and November.

Take I-75 to Griffin exit. Turn right onto Ga. 19/41 and carry on 14 miles. Raceway is on right.

Dirt Tracks

Dixie Speedway Highway 92 Woodstock	Stock car	Sat. nights, spring-summer	926-5315
Senoia Speedway Highway 16 (3 mi. W. of Senoia) Senoia	Stock car	Sat. nights, spring-summer	1-599-3513
West Atlanta Raceway 2984 Warren Rd. Douglasville	Stock car	Fri. nights, spring-summer	942-8660

196

XII

SPECIAL PEOPLE

At the Zoo

KIDS' STUFF

It's after school, the weekend, vacation. . . and the kids are bored.
At these trying moments, parental action is urgently called for. But what to do? Here's an alphabet for the perplexed parent.

A is for Animals

Grant Park Zoo in Atlanta's Grant Park houses a collection of strange beasts. Monkeys chatter, rhinos ruminate, giraffes gyrate, reptiles slither, and sea-lions play while the great cats — lions and tigers — prowl on padded feet. But Willie B., the big gorilla, prefers his own TV set to these companions. Open: M - Sun., 10 am - 5 pm. Closed: Dec. 25, Jan. 1. Entrance fee.
Stone Mountain Game Ranch in Stone Mountain Park has a small group of deer and other wildlife species.
Open: 10 am - 9 pm, summer; 10 am - 5:30 pm, rest of year. Entrance fee.

B is for Babysitters

But not just any babysitters — Supersitters! With certificates to prove it.
The certificates are awarded by Scottish Rite Hospital in Sandy Springs, which sponsors regular babysitting clinics for teenagers. The clinics last two hours, and cover topics such as basic and emergency child care, safety precautions, essential information, and ways to keep children busy and happy. At the end of the clinic students take a test, and, if they pass it, are awarded supersitter status.
Parents needing trained babysitters may call the hospital (tel.: 256-3535). Their names and addresses will be passed on to graduates of the program.

THE INSIDER'S ATLANTA

C is for Cars...

The General Motors Assembly Plant, 3900 Motors Industrial Way, Doraville, (tel.: 455-5254) offers tours that enable you to see how a car is made. Children should be accompanied by an adult, and if there are more than five in your party, advance reservations are requested.

Tours: M - F, 8:30 am and 12:30 pm. Free.

...And Creativity...

Many local Parks and Recreation Departments offer arts and crafts classes for children. Contact the one in your county or city to find out what's available. Among the best are the programs offered by the Chastain Park Arts and Crafts Center, 135 West Wieuca Road, N.E., in Atlanta and Callanwolde Fine Arts Center, 980 Briarcliff Road, N.E., in DeKalb.

The annual Children's Festival sponsored by the Atlanta Arts Alliance brings fun aplenty to the Memorial Arts Center each February. There are musicians, actors, clowns, mimes, puppets, dancers, and a host of other activities to keep little people busy.

...And the Cyclorama

This giant work — it weighs seven tons — is a circular painting depicting with life-size figures the hard-fought Battle of Atlanta that marked the climax of the Civil War. First displayed in its Grant Park location in 1898, the Cyclorama was recently restored. Visitors are now able to watch the dramatic conflict unfold from a slowly-rotating central viewing gallery.

Open daily, 9 am — 5 pm. Admission fee.

D is for Drama

There is a thriving children's theatre in Atlanta. Here's a list of companies that regularly perform for children.

Company	Location	Telephone
Academy Children's Theatre	Academy Theatre 1137 Peachtree St., NE	873-2518
Academy Theatre Artists-in-Schools	Schools statewide	873-2518
Atlanta Children's Theatre	Alliance Theatre 1280 Peachtree St., NE	892-2414

Umbrella Players (Alliance Theatre)   Schools statewide   898-1132

E is for Excitement!

They call **Six Flags Over Georgia** the land of screams and dreams. It's a place where you defy gravity, logic and every instinct of self-preservation. You can be dropped to earth by parachute from a point many stories above the ground, whirled around upside down, swished into a river at high speed, hurtled up, down and round steel rails on the ultimate rollercoasters, the triple-loop Mind Bender and the Great American Scream Machine, and swung madly to and fro in the Flying Dutchman. The new Monster Plantation will make you moan, while Thunder River shoots you through raging torrents. For those whose stomachs are not strong enough for such fare, there are two music halls and live entertainment.

Open: March - May, Sat. & Sun.; May - Sept. 1, M - Sun.; Sept. 2 - Nov., Sat. & Sun.

Take I-20W to Six Flags exit.

F is for Farm

The DeKalb Extension Service has a small farm at its Environmental Studies Center, 2390 Wildcat Road, Decatur (tel.: 241-7444). Here you can feed billy and nanny goats and their kids, discover how clever pigs and piglets are, and go up close to horses, chickens and donkeys. You'll learn a lot about all these animals too. Groups of 10 - 25 are preferred.

Open: M - F; tours must be scheduled.

Take I-20E to Candler Road (Highway 155) exit. Right on Candler Road. Keep right at fork (Panthersville Road), then right at first light (Clifton Springs Road) and left on Wildcat Road. Center's office is stone building on right.

G is for The General

This famous locomotive, which was involved in The Great Atlanta Locomotive Chase, is now on display at Kennesaw Mountain National Battlefield Park, in the Big Shanty Museum. (Open: M - Sun., 9 am - 6 pm.) The other locomotive in the chase, the *Texas,* is on display at the Cyclorama.

The Great Atlanta Locomotive Chase took place in the thick of the Civil War. A daring band of Yankee soldiers had made their way South to steal a Confederate engine, ride it north, and blow up all the railway bridges between Atlanta and Chattanooga. This would destroy the Confederates' line of supply.

On April 22, 1862 the raiders struck. They hijacked the *General* at the Big Shanty station while the guards and passengers were eating and headed north at top speed.

When the Confederates realized what had happened, they gave chase as fast as they could in whatever they could find until they came across another locomotive, the *Texas.* Then they used the *Texas* to try and catch the Yankees before they could blow up any bridges.

The *Texas* was more powerful than the *General,* and the Yankees were delayed by various things, and soon the Confederates had the Yankees in sight. Just five miles from Chattanooga, the *General* ran out of fuel, and the raiders were forced to escape, their mission unsuccessful. Eventually many were captured, and their leader, James A. Andrews, and seven others were hanged on Peachtree Street — a sad end to a bold venture.

H is for the High Museum. . .

A special exhibit for children entitled *Spaces and Illusions* is on display at the High Museum, 1280 Peachtree Street, NE (tel.: 892-3600). It demonstrates, with holograms, trompe l'oeil techniques, and other methods, how art can deceive the eye into taking appearance for reality.

. . . and 4-H Clubs. . .

The H's stand for Head, Heart, Hands and Health. 4-H Clubs are organized by your county Extension Service and funded by the U.S. Department of Agriculture. They enable kids from 5th grade through high school to select a group project to work on, and to receive training manuals and literature from the County Extension Service. The more than 40 subjects from which kids can choose a project range from caring for animals to rocketry. Most 4-H clubs are organized through the school systems, but if there isn't one in your child's school and you have a group of kids eager to join, contact your extension service about starting one. Most projects are educational, but many are just fun.

. . . and Homework

Kids having trouble with their homework can now find expert assistance over the telephone. Sponsored by the Atlanta school system, the CARE line (tel.: 761-5404) operates Monday through Thursday from 5 to 8 p.m. CARE stands for Call A Resource in Education, and the resources who man the phones are highly qualified teachers skilled in English, math, social science, and science.

J is for Junior Ranger

The Georgia Department of Natural Resources (tel.: 656-7092) has created a Junior Ranger program for kids between the ages of 8 and 14. The real fun comes in qualifying for a Junior Ranger badge. To do so, a child must visit at least one historic site in Georgia and participate in two nature-oriented programs sponsored by the Department. Then he fills out a report card. After he has qualified, parents and children take part in a special, once a year camp-out to celebrate. Children can renew their membership each year by taking part in other activities.

L is for Library

Kids can expand their world through books borrowed from the children's sections of Atlanta's public library systems. Many libraries also offer story-hours when children can listen to tales of high adventure skilfully told. Contact the library nearest you for details.

M is for Money...

Lots of it! Some may look a little strange — like conch shells and beads — but there's nothing weird about solid gold bars. It's all on display in the Monetary Museum at the Federal Reserve Bank, 104 Marietta Street, in downtown Atlanta. Appointments are required (tel.: 586-8747).

...and Music...

Whether your child is a prodigy or not, if he has come musical talent, Atlanta offers him a number of opportunities to perform, including a symphony orchestra and choral groups. These are listed below. Also consult your Parks and Recreation Department.

Group	Age	Audition	Aud'n Date	Tours	Tuition	Telephone
Atlanta Boy Choir	5-7, 7-13	Yes	Jan.,Sept.	Yes, abroad and in U.S.	Yes	Fletcher Wolfe, 378-0064
Atlanta Symphony Youth Orchestra	14 yrs.- 12 grade	Yes	Mid Sept.	No	Yes	898-1177

Allow yourself at least three weeks to practice for this audition. Concerts are given in fall, winter and spring. For the winter one, members of the youth orchestra will be selected to appear as soloists. Eight scholarships for further musical training are awarded to outstanding members of the orchestra.

Cobb County "Young Artist" Series	Young adult	Yes	By arrange-ment	No	No	Elizabeth Marsden, 422-3500

This series of solo performances, sponsored by the Cobb County Arts Council, is open to outstanding young artists in five categories: voice, piano, other instrumental, ballet, and drama. There is also a visual arts program.

Cobb Youth Chorale	6-14	Yes	By arrange-ment	Yes	Yes; scholar-ships available	Elizabeth Kimble, 355-0179

Young Singers of Callanwolde	4th-8th grade	Yes	April-May	Yes, abroad and in U.S.	Yes	873-1708/ 872-5338

Atlanta also offers some excellent opportunities for you to introduce your child to classical music.

The nationally acclaimed **Atlanta Symphony Orchestra** presents special programs designed to do just that. Coffee Concerts, given at Symphony Hall on selected Saturday mornings throughout the year, enable your whole family to enjoy the orchestra at reduced prices. Call 892-2414 for information. And don't forget the special Family Christmas Concert given every year in December; it's just right for the festive season.

Also at Symphony Hall are the Young People's Concerts for elementary and high school kids. But the ASO's Symphony Street programs for pre-schoolers through second-graders come out to you, and are given in neighborhood halls. For information about these two programs, call 892-3600. They're informal, often organized around themes, and different aspects of the orchestra are fully explained.

The **Atlanta Community Orchestra** also presents special Kinder Concerts from time to time. The music is accompanied by dancing, slides, or other visual effects to make the concerts even more enjoyable. For information, call the Atlanta Music Club (tel.: 233-2131).

... and Museums

Why, oh why, in a city as big and rich as Atlanta, with so many research institutions, universities and high-technology industries, is there no real museum in the region?

Apart from Fernbank Science Center, described under S for Science, only the museum in the State Capitol comes close. Emory University has an extensive collection of Egyptian mummies and Mesopotamian clay tablets, ancient pottery fragments from the Holy Land, Indian relics, and a fine collection of prints, drawings, and photographs; but these will not be on display until renovation of the Old Law Building is complete in 1984, and the new Emory Museum of Art and Archaeology is revealed. Until then, try the **Georgia State Museum of Science and Industry** (tel.: 656-2844) on the fourth floor of the State Capitol. Here are displayed over 500 wildlife species in natural habitats, as well as Georgia minerals and various artifacts.

Open: M-F, 8 am - 5:30 pm.

N is for Nature

Special environmental programs for kids are offered at Panola Mountain State Park, the Chattahoochee Nature Center, the Outdoor Activity Center, the W. H. Reynolds Nature Preserve, Providence Road Park, and Wildwood Park. For details, see "Best Foot Forward" in Part X.

P is for Pets...

If your pooch or pussycat must be pedigreed, there are plenty of pet-shops in Atlanta to sell you just the breed you need. Also check the classified ads.

But if all you want is a warm and lovable bundle of fur, you'll find a variety of little creatures that fit the bill at the Atlanta Humane Society's two adoption centers at 981 Howell Mill Road, N.W. (corner of 10th Street) and 3625 Peachtree Road, N.E.

... and Playing...

Most neighborhood parks have jungle gyms, slides, swings, and other paraphernalia that need only a child's imagination to be transformed into fantasylands.

One of the best playgrounds is the Isamu Noguchi-designed *PLAYSCAPES* erected by the High Museum of Art in Piedmont Park.

... and Puppets

Puppetry has reached the state of a high art in Atlanta, largely through the efforts of those who helped create the Center for Puppetry Arts, 1404 Spring Street corner 18th Street, in Atlanta (tel.: 873-3391). Here the Vagabond Marionettes will enthrall both children and their parents with their wide repertoire of fairy tales and beloved children's stories. And don't forget to visit the attached puppetry museum, supposedly the most complete in the southeast.

S is for Science and the Stars. . .

Twinkle, twinkle little star,
How I wonder what you are!

Every child knows that rhyme, and at Fernbank Science Center's Planetarium and Observatory he'll have a chance to find the answer to the riddle. The closest thing to a scientific museum in Atlanta, Fernbank also has an exhibition hall where objects of natural history, including a moon rock, and the Apollo 6 Command Module are on display. Fernbank is supported by the DeKalb County School System, but most of its services are open to all.

Open: Planetarium programs, Tu. - F., 8 pm; Sat., 11 am & 3 pm; Sun., 3 pm; Observatory, Th., F., 8 - 10:30 pm when skies clear, 8-9:30 pm if clouded; Exhibit Hall, M, Sat., 8:30 am - 5 pm; Tu-F., 8:30 am - 10 pm; Sun., 1:30 - 5 pm.

Fernbank is located at 156 Heaton Drive, NE (off Artwood Road, off Ponce de Leon Avenue) (tel.: 378-4311). To find out about Fernbank's other educational services, turn to the education section of this book.

. . . and Scouts

Being prepared is fun for boys and girls and their parents.

To find out about the boy scout troop in your area, contact the Atlanta Area Council of the Boy Scouts of America (tel.: 577-4810). Scout troops fall into three age categories: Cub scouts, 8-10 years; Boy scouts, 11-15 years; Explorer programs for boys and girls, 16-21 years. The Explorer program is career oriented and a number of businesses and institutions participate in it.

For information about Girl Scout programs in your area, contact the Northwest Georgia Council (tel.: 522-1160), which organizes troops for girls from first grade through high school.

T is for Toys

One of the nicest recent additions to the lives of Atlanta's children, the **Toy Museum**, 2800 Peachtree Road, NE (tel.: 266-8697) is an old house that has been converted into a treasure trove of playthings that will delight and intrigue kids and their parents. The Museum claims to have over 100,000 toys on display. Many are antiques, and all are exhibited in environments of the period.

Open: M-Sat., 10 am - 5 pm; Sun., 2 - 5 pm. Entrance fee. Birthday facilities.

Don't forget the **Victorian Playhouse** at the Atlanta Historical Society,

Playscapes

3099 Andrews Drive N.W. You can't go in, but you can peep through glass windows into a miniature mansion filled with playthings lovingly preserved by yesterday's children, now grown old.

... and Trains

The **Southeastern Railway Museum** between Norcross and Duluth, is sure to interest youngsters, who can climb into the old cabooses, carriages and engines and pretend to be brakemen and guards. You'll find the Museum described in the chapter on Getting Around.

For a real train ride in a miniature train, catch the **Stone Mountain Scenic Railroad**; it's slow but steady.

U is for Update

Consult the newspaper's Saturday *Weekend* section for weekly information on activities for children in the "What's Up for Kids" column.

W is for Wren's Nest

The Wren's Nest, 1050 Gordon Street, SW, was the home of Joel Chandler Harris, creator of the Uncle Remus legends and the enchanting tales of Tar Baby, Bre'r Rabbit and company. The house is full of the author's memorabilia.

Open: M-Sat., 9:30 am - 5 pm; Sun., 2 - 5 pm. Entrance fee.

Z is for Ze Rest

Many of the activities described in other parts of this book will also appeal to children. For example, kids' sports are described in the chapter, Good Sport! Most kids would also enjoy the historical and outdoor excursions listed elsewhere. Finally, there is special provision for children during events like the Atlanta Arts Festival held in Piedmont Park each year in May. One treat that kids stand in line for is to have their faces beautifully painted to resemble fairies, clowns, and butterflies.

Ze Rest is also dedicated to the activities you will undoubtedly invent in those desperate times when nothing at all seems to amuse. We wish you many happy inspirations!

WOMAN
TO
WOMAN

Georgia is not a state that is big on women's issues. The fate of the Equal Rights Amendment, which has been defeated in the General Assembly every time it was introduced, is proof of that.

Nevertheless, a number of organizations formed by and for women exist in Atlanta. Some enable women to participate actively in civic life. Others assist women to move upward in the job market by providing them with contacts and skills. Still another approaches female health care from a feminist viewpoint.

Here's a brief introduction to some of the most active of these organizations.

The Women's Chamber of Commerce

The Women's Chamber of Commerce provides a means by which women working at all levels in the business world can play an active role in community affairs, as well as gain information of use to them in their careers.

Through its various committees, the Chamber works toward the beautification of the city by planting trees, supports cultural programs, and sponsors educational programs that assist working women. The Chamber's most important project is the week-long *Dogwood Festival*, which it sponsors every year in April, a time which coincides with the blooming season of the city's famous dogwood trees.

For more information, contact the Women's Chamber of Commerce, Suite 540, 33 North Avenue, N. E., Atlanta, Georgia 30308 (tel.: 892-0538).

Feminist Action Alliance

The Feminist Action Alliance (tel.: 872-7544) is an organization that concentrates on specific issues affecting women. Its employment task force sponsors a "Women at Work" conference every year, "non-traditional career days" at high schools, and other programs. Among the other issues the Alliance has addressed are family and health services, and ways to assist women to enter politics.

Closely related to the Feminist Action Alliance is the **Atlanta Women's Network** (tel.: 577-5635). This organization was founded in the belief that many men have reached the top of their professions by means of the old boy network: that business and advancement have come to them partly because of what they know, but even more because of whom they know. The Atlanta Women's Network is an attempt to create a similar range of contacts for professional women, by means of monthly luncheon meetings addressed by influential women who share their experiences and contacts.

The YWCA Midtown Women's Center

"Where the W makes the difference," says the YWCA's slogan, and at the Midtown Center it certainly does.

Operating out of an old house located at 45 11th Street N.E., the Center (tel.: 892-3476) offers a number of services specifically geared to women.

Among these special services is a legal clinic staffed by women attorneys where, for a minimal fee, advice is available on a wide range of legal problems, including divorce, child support, and property rights.

The Feminist Women's Health Center

This organization is described in the chapter, "A Healthy Mind in a Healthy Body."

The League of Women Voters

Don't be misled by the name; men **are** eligible to take part in this organization.

The League's purpose is to encourage informed participation in the political process. It does this in two ways: by promoting voter registration, and by studying and preparing pamphlets on issues of concern to voters in Georgia. The League has chapters in Atlanta-Fulton, DeKalb, Cobb-Marietta, and Gwinnett. These chapters concentrate on issues affecting local government and on matters requiring action by the Georgia General Assembly. A national convention of the League is held each year at which national policy concerns are discussed.

For more information, contact the League of Women Voters of Georgia, 3272 Peachtree Road, N.E. (tel.: 237-9294).

SPECIAL PEOPLE

The American Association of University Women (AAUW)

Membership in the AAUW (tel.: 451-2024) is open to all women who are college graduates, and its activities are heavily oriented toward education. The organization sponsors a variety of educational programs for its members and supports a scholarship fund for women university students — primarily through its annual Used Book Sale held at Lenox Square in September. AAUW also maintains an **Educational Information and Referral Service** (tel.: 233-7497) which is open to all at no cost. This service provides information on degree programs, financial aid, and other opportunities offered by universities and colleges in Atlanta and other Georgia cities. Career counseling is also available. The service operates Mondays through Thursdays from 10 a.m. to 5 p.m. Its offices are in the Professional Concourse, Lenox Square (between Davison's and Neiman-Marcus).

The Georgia Executive Women's Network

This organization is open exclusively to women who have been in a management position at a decision-making level for at least two years, and to professional women like lawyers and accountants.

Its purpose is to foster the careers of executive women and to enable younger women to meet and learn from older women in senior positions.

Meetings are held regularly, and seminars and workshops for members are presented. Some are open to the public.

For information, write to: The Georgia Executive Women's Network, P. O. Box 80195, Atlanta, Ga. 30346 (tel.: 396-1420).

The Women's Commerce Club

Long excluded from membership in some of Atlanta's private business clubs, women in Atlanta have retaliated by founding their own.

Claimed to be the first in the nation, the Women's Commerce Club offers members an elegant environment in which to entertain clients and meet other professional women. Located at 1112 Peachtree Street, N.E., the club's facilities include dining and conference rooms as well as recreational amenities.

Application materials may be obtained by writing: Women's Commerce Club, P.O. Box 18724, Atlanta, Ga. 30326.

SILVER THREADS
AMONG THE GOLD

Senior citizenship need not mean retirement into a world of lavender and old lace. Instead, with some of the freebies provided by state and local governments, it can open up new vistas of education and activity.

You're Never Too Old to Learn

Especially when you can earn a degree absolutely free. Since 1977, the Board of Regents of the University System of Georgia has made it possible for persons 62 years of age or older to do just that at any college within the system. In Atlanta, that means you can attend Georgia State University, Georgia Tech, Kennesaw College, or Clayton Junior College at no cost.

There are some restrictions: space must be available in the class you wish to attend, and the provision does not apply to medical, dental, law and veterinary schools; and some qualifications: age, and ability to satisfy the normal academic entry requirements. But if you clear those hurdles, you're home free.

Emory University, which is not part of the University System, has created a special program for retired professionals, the Senior University. Classes are conducted by members who have special knowledge in a particular field, and there are also seminars and discussion groups. The object is to create "an environment where members can pursue their intellectual interests, develop new interests, and engage in dialogue with other similarly minded retired professionals." There is a tuition fee of $100 a year. For information, telephone 329-6000, or write: Emory's Senior University, Community Educational Services, Emory University, Atlanta, Georgia 30322.

212

Workin'

If you're retired and don't want to be, contact the Golden Age Employment Service, 34 Tenth Street, N.E., Atlanta (tel.: 881-5998).

You might also consider volunteering. Many services are in urgent need of willing assistants. For information, contact Volunteer Atlanta (tel.: 522-0110), Volunteer DeKalb (tel.: 451-1376), Volunteer Cobb-Douglas (tel.: 428-8344), or the United Way office in your area.

Having Fun

The Atlanta Public Library System schedules special film series for senior citizens. Contact the branch nearest you for details.

Many county and city Parks and Recreation Departments also offer special programs and classes for senior citizens, as do County Extension Services. Special fitness classes for senior citizens are offered at many YWCAs and YMCAs.

You can enjoy adventures in learning about car-care, creative writing, ballroom dancing, swimming, and many other topics through Life Enrichment Services, 3715 LaVista Road, Decatur (tel.: 321-6960).

Information

Your one-stop source of information on matters relating to the elderly is the Golden Age Information and Referral Service, 34 Tenth Street, N.E., Atlanta, Georgia 30309 (tel.: 881-5977). Open: M-F, 9 am - 5 pm. A similar office is located at 202 Nelson Ferry Road, Decatur, Ga. 30030 (tel.: 377-9901).

Legal Tangles

The **Senior Citizens Law Project** (tel.: 524-5811) is a program that enables senior citizens, especially those with low incomes, to assert their rights in a variety of legal matters. These include problems with social security, food stamps, Medicaid, housing, and consumer issues. Through the Project, persons over 60 can obtain free legal representation in these and other civil cases. The Project operates in Fulton, DeKalb, Cobb, Gwinnett, and Clayton Counties.

Through the Project, senior citizens with moderate incomes can also obtain referrals to lawyers in the Atlanta area who have agreed to charge the elderly reduced rates for legal services.

A similar program is also available through the State Bar of Georgia's **Elderly Referral Panel**. By calling a statewide toll-free number (tel.: 1-800-282-5851), persons over 60 with incomes of less than $15,000 a year will be referred to attorneys throughout the state. These attorneys have agreed to provide a first consultation free, and further services at reduced fees.

XIII

A HEALTHY MIND
IN
A HEALTHY BODY

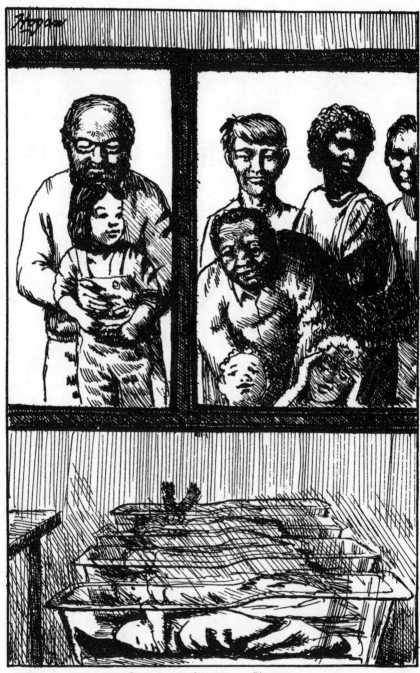

Newborns, Northside Hospital

MEDICAL
ALTERNATIVES

There are, according to the Atlanta Chamber of Commerce, 56 licensed hospitals, more than 3,500 physicians, and 900 dentists in the Atlanta metropolitan area.

But sometimes you don't want to see a doctor. You'd just like some information. Maybe you'd prefer a less traditional health environment than a doctor's office or a hospital. Perhaps you'd prefer to cut your health care costs.

This chapter introduces you to ways of accomplishing all three objectives.

Tel-Med

Should you send your ailing child to school? How would you recognize the early warnings of a heart attack or the symptoms of hepatitis, and where should you turn for help? How should you care for a patient in your home, and how could you learn to apply mouth to mouth resuscitation in an emergency?

Answers to these questions and some 150 others are as close as your telephone. They're available from Tel-Med, a telephone health library for the public.

Tel-Med was inaugurated in Atlanta in 1974 by the DeKalb Medical Society and is sponsored in cooperation with DeKalb General Hospital.

It consists of a carefully-screened collection of tapes dealing with such topics as arthritis, birth control, cancer, home patient care, children's diseases, dental care, diseases of the digestive system, drug and alcohol abuse treatment, first aid, heart ailments, parenting, plastic surgery, pregnancy, respiratory illness, skin disorders, smoking, and venereal diseases.

You can obtain this information by calling Tel-Med (tel.: 296-9000) and requesting by number the tape you require. Tel-Med will also send you free a list

217

of tapes available, with their numbers. The service operates Monday through Friday from noon to 8 pm.

Survival Skills

You may not be a scout, but you'd still like to be prepared. The American Red Cross (tel.: 881-9800) offers a number of classes to help you achieve your goal. Instruction is provided in first aid techniques, cardiopulmonary resuscitation (CPR), methods of monitoring your own vital signs (like blood pressure), parenting, and home nursing, including care of patients suffering from multiple sclerosis.

Emergency Room Alternatives

Now there is an alternative to the hospital emergency room. Several groups of physicians have established clinics that offer emergency medical treatment in cases that do not require an overnight stay in hospital. Doctors undertake minor surgery, hospital emergency room treatment, and many services a general practitioner might perform. Appointments are not required.

Most of these clinics are listed in the Yellow Pages under "Physicians and Surgeons Emergency Service."

Birthing

In some cultures, women have babies and return to their household tasks within a few hours. In our own, until quite recently, birth was considered a painful process which the mother could escape through unconsciousness. Now, however, many regard birth as an almost mystical experience in which the whole family should share.

If you fall into this third category, consider the **Birthing Room** of the Douglas General Hospital (tel.: 949-1500) in Douglasville for your next baby. Procedures here differ from conventional hospital births in many ways. The mother is attended by a nurse-midwife (and/or a physician), both her husband and their other children may be present, parents are encouraged to handle the baby, which remains with the mother, as soon as it is born, and the mother may be discharged within 12 hours of delivery. If the mother's stay in the hospital is less than 12 hours, she may find the cost of the stay substantially lower than in conventional maternity hospitals. To make use of the birthing center, you must be a patient of physicians connected with the hospital.

Most maternity hospitals in the metro area offer classes in the fundamentals of childbirth for nervous parents-to-be. Other organizations that provide instruction in these matters are the *LaMaze Association of Atlanta* (tel.: 881-8670) which gives lessons in natural childbirth, and the *Red Cross* (tel.: 881-

A HEALTHY MIND IN A HEALTHY BODY

9800) which offers free classes for new parents that cover delivery and care of the newborn. Some YMCA's also give pre-natal fitness classes that help pregnant ladies shape up. And, if you are interested in breast-feeding your baby, the *La Leche League* (tel.: 636-8454) offers instruction and encouragement.

Conquering Cancer

Information about cancer, its treatment, and local services, is available free from the Georgia Cancer Information Service (tel.: 1-800-327-7332). The service operates Monday through Friday from 9 am - 4:30 pm.

The Feminist Women's Health Center

Founded in 1977 as an outgrowth of the Women's Movement, the Feminist Women's Health Center, 580 14th Street, N.W., is an attempt to enable women to make informed decisions about the medical treatment they wish to receive.

The Center is owned and operated by women — one of 26 such clinics in the nation. Its services include pregnancy screening, abortion services, a "self-help clinic" or series of health education lectures on topics affecting women, and "well-woman" gynaecology services. These last include birth control information and various procedures requiring lab tests. Lay persons staff the "well woman" clinic. They do not prescribe, but attempt to provide women patients with enough information about alternative treatments to enable the patients to choose the appropriate one for themselves. Abortions are performed by doctors.

The Center is open Monday through Saturday from 9 am to 6 pm (tel.: 874-7551).

GRADY

To most Atlantans, the name Grady Hospital is synonymous with welfare and the poor, and therefore a topic about which it is almost mandatory to complain.

In reality, Grady is a little like one of those Chinese puzzle boxes that when opened reveal boxes within boxes.

Within its unprepossessing exterior, Grady houses no fewer than 11 compartments of specialized medical services, in addition to five health-related professional schools, and training facilities for young physicians. Grady's departments are headed by physicians on the faculty of Emory University Medical School.

The majority of its patients use Grady because they are unable to afford medical care elsewhere. But Grady also has the state's only Category I emergency center, made up of five separate units able to provide 24-hour care in any medical crisis. Its Regional Perinatal Center provides medical care for high-risk mothers and newborn babies, and Angel Two, Grady's specially equipped nursery on wheels, can rush babies to hospital for treatment in an emergency. The largest diabetes clinic in the U.S. is at Grady, and it pioneered a diet therapy approach which reduces costs and hospitalizations.

Grady also has a separate Burn Unit, a Poison Control Center providing instant advice by telephone on how to treat cases of poisoning, a Regional Nephrology Center performing kidney dialysis and transplants, a Cystic Fibrosis Center, a Family Planning Program, a Nurse-Wifery Service, a Hand Clinic, and several outpatient clinics inside and outside the hospital structure.

In a typical year, Grady admits 40,000 patients to its 1,000 beds, and handles some 750,000 outpatient cases, including some 250,000 emergencies. For thousands, the hospital has taken the place of the family doctor.

A HEALTHY MIND IN A HEALTHY BODY

The Rape Crisis Center

The hospital also maintains a 24-hour emergency hotline providing counseling and assistance to women who have been raped and to their families. The number is 659-7273 (659-RAPE). The hotline is part of Grady's **Rape Crisis Center,** which serves more than 1,000 victims a year with psychological and legal assistance.

Grady is named for Henry W. Grady, famed editor of *The Atlanta Constitution,* who championed the cause of a public hospital in Atlanta until his death in 1889. Since Grady's death, support for the cause has dwindled to no more than lukewarm. The hospital's budget is an annual source of controversy. An equally hoary perennial is the question of who should pay for Grady – the taxpayers of Fulton and DeKalb counties, who now foot most of Grady's bills, or the state, which benefits from Grady's training facilities and from whose rural areas many of Grady's patients are drawn.

It may take another Henry Grady to keep Grady's services at their current level, but as long as the sick stream in at the door, there will be room in Atlanta for the hospital he envisioned.

Have Cure,

At the Center for Disease Control, near Emory, researchers probing the minute organisms that cause disease and death have helped stamp out old diseases like smallpox and find cures for new ones.

CDC's activities cross national boundaries to serve the world. They have even gone beyond this world; when man went to the moon, CDC cooperated with NASA to prevent the spread of earthly diseases to the moon, or moonly diseases on earth.

It was CDC researchers who identified the bacterium that caused the mysterious Legionnaire's Disease that struck down convention delegates in Philadelphia in 1978. A special squad of CDC epidemiologists, the Epidemic Intelligence Service, stands ready at any moment to fly to remote corners of the globe on the track of killer diseases.

The CDC started out in 1946 as a center for the investigation and control of malaria. Today, it is one of six major agencies of the U.S. Public Health Service. Its responsibilities include seeking the causes and cures of diseases carried by any organism, not just mosquitoes, as well as the study of infectious diseases, leukaemia, con-

Information and

The agencies listed here provide comprehensive information on services and facilities meeting specialized needs in the Atlanta area.

Agency	Telephone
Atlanta Area Services for the Blind, Inc. 763 Peachtree St., N.E., Atlanta, Ga. 30308	875-9011
Georgia Association for Retarded Citizens, Inc. 1851 Ram Runway, Suite 104, College Park, Ga. 30337	761-3150

Will Travel

genital defects, and the effect of smoking and diet on health. Other important areas of study are methods of controlling the spread of diseases in hospitals and of reducing occupational health hazards.

CDC's extensive laboratory facilities include a new, special Maximum Containment Laboratory. Here scientists, working through gloves projecting into a glassed-in isolation booth, can study viruses that are too dangerous to be handled in an ordinary lab. A number of CDC's laboratories have been designated by the World Health Organization as international reference centers.

Among CDC's achievements have been the pioneering use of fluorescent antibody techniques in the diagnosis of various diseases, the successful culturing of a leprosy bacillus, and important discoveries about viruses that cause disease. CDC also supplies rare vaccines and drugs that are not commercially produced.

It is likely that CDC's job will never be done. For as old diseases are eliminated, new ones are added: drug-resistant tuberculosis and gonorrhea, new types of hepatitis, diseases caused by industrially-generated poisons and radiation.

For CDC scientists, daybreak is always just beyond the horizon.

Referral Agencies

Georgia Association for the Deaf/   876-2117
Georgia Registry of Interpreters for the Deaf
1182 W. Peachtree St., Suite 213, Atlanta, Ga. 30309

Mental Health Association, Metro Atlanta Chapter   522-9910
100 Edgewood Ave., N.E., Suite 502, Atlanta, Ga. 30303

How To Be
Wholly Healthy

I'm not sick, but am I as well as I could be? That's the question many Atlantans are asking as they turn to "holistic" healing methods that seek to bring body and mind into a harmony that enhances health.

Some holistic techniques simply involve changes in nutritional patterns, exercise and lifestyle. Others find the key to health in such rites as accupressure, iridology, and rolfing.

For the unitiated, these healing techniques translate respectively into: massage upon meridians or points of energy within the body to release stress; the technique of photographing and reading the nerve endings in the iris of the eye to show the strengths and weaknesses of the body; and a technique for reordering the body to approach an ideal in which the left and front sides are more nearly balanced and the pelvis approaches horizontal.

If none of these methods seems right for you, don't despair. There are many others to choose from, like Reiki healing in which energy is directed through the hands to cure disease, psychosynthesis, synergy, past life regression therapy, and applied kinesiology.

Of course, it may just be that your attitude is wrong. In that case, you may need an awareness initiator to make you aware of yourself and your universe, or even a specialist in color awareness to show you that color is energy.

You'll find practitioners of all these arts listed in the bimonthly *Natural Health Guide*, available free at health food stores and public libraries.

CUTTING
HEALTH CARE
COSTS

You've been early to bed and early to rise, and still you're not too healthy, not too wealthy, and not too sure of the wise way out of your predicament.

Relax! Health care need not bankrupt you if you explore some of the alternatives Atlanta has to offer.

The County Clinic

The mission of the county health department is to prevent you from getting sick, and, in a few cases, to treat you if you do.

One of the jobs of county health officials is to protect the environment. To this end, they snoop around restaurant kitchens on the watch for unhygienic practices that could make you sick. They are the scourge of rats, roaches, mosquitoes and disease-bearing denizens of the urban jungle. They monitor radiation and air and water pollution levels in the metropolitan air.

From the public's point of view, these activities are conducted behind the scenes by faceless individuals. But the second part of the health department's activities involve face-to-face encounters with John Q. Citizen.

Some of these encounters are in the public schools, where health officials periodically test students' speech, hearing and vision.

Others are in county-run physical health clinics where a wide variety of medical services are offered.

Here county residents can receive free immunization against disease (including inoculations required for children and for foreign travel), screenings for diabetes, high blood pressure and other chronic diseases as well as cancer, family-planning services, and health check-ups for well children under the age of five. Counties also administer maternal care programs for pregnant women meeting

225

certain income guidelines, as well as limited dental care programs.

While the goal of these programs is prevention rather than cure, counties do provide treatment as well as diagnosis for tuberculosis, sexually-transmitted diseases and alcoholism.

There are public health clinics in all the metropolitan counties, with 12 in DeKalb and 24 in Fulton. Not all services are provided at all clinics, so check with the one nearest you before you schedule an appointment. Most programs are open to all county residents, irrespective of income. Many are free; however, a charge based on income is made for family planning and "well-child" clinic services.

Dentistry

Dentists in Atlanta are no shyer than their medical colleagues of charging staggering sums for their services. But you can avoid having your purse as well as your teeth drawn by making use of Emory University's School of Dentistry dental clinics, 1462 Clifton Road, N.E. (tel.: 329-6710).

Here a full range of dental services is provided by juniors and seniors in the School of Dentistry, working under expert supervision. Fees charged are from one-half to one-third less than regular dental fees, and there is no charge for an initial evaluation of the problem. However, you will be accepted for treatment only if there is a student requiring practice on your type of complaint.

COUNTY
MENTAL HEALTH
PROGRAMS

Loneliness, alienation, anxiety, the sense of being unable to cope — these are symptoms of life in any 20th century metropolis, and sometimes they seem to overwhelm the possibility of happiness.

Fortunately, it is not necessary to fight these bugbears unaided. Inexpensive professional help is available in many parts of the metro area in mental health centers created by county health departments. There are three major centers in DeKalb and five in Fulton, as well as centers in Cobb, Clayton, Gwinnett and other counties.

Mental health services provided cover the spectrum from counseling through crisis intervention and treatment for alcohol and drug addiction to training of the severely retarded.

Counseling Services

County mental health centers offer help and counseling for depression, domestic or adolescent problems, nervousness, anxiety, and mental confusion. Some counties offer special programs for troubled children or adolescents, and a few provide in-patient services through associated area hospitals. Counseling is provided to individuals, families, or groups by trained psychologists.

You do not need a referral to use the services of mental health centers. Appointments are preferred, except in an emergency. Patients are charged on a sliding fee scale based on income and family size.

The five counties also maintain emergency 24-hour telephone numbers manned by trained personnel who provide counseling or referrals in a crisis.

All five counties maintain centers for alcohol and drug addiction where counseling, detoxification and treatment are available. Some include short-term residential facilities.

Services for the Mentally Retarded

County health departments provide important services for the mentally retarded. These services range from diagnosis to provision of residential facilities.

Diagnosis and evaluation of suspected cases of retardation are performed by teams consisting of a social worker, a nurse, a speech and hearing specialist, a physician, and a psychologist.

All five counties operate training centers where retarded individuals, according to their ability, are taught vocational and/or "survival" skills. These facilities serve pre-schoolers and adults. By law, children in the 5 to 18 year age group are the responsibility of the public school systems.

Counties also maintain sex-segregated residential facilities for the retarded, and many either have, or are developing, community residence programs which enable retarded persons who do not require institutionalization to be placed in homes in the community. Gwinnett County also has a "Respite" program which accommodates retarded children when their parents wish to go away on vacation.

County Health Departments

County	Physical Health	Mental Health
Cobb	422-9440	424-0870
Clayton	471-8635	991-0111
DeKalb	294-3700	292-5231
Fulton	572-2751	572-2961
Gwinnett) Rockdale) Newton)	963-6136	963-8141

COUNSELING
SERVICES

If life is getting you down, you're fighting with your spouse, your kids think you don't understand them (and you don't), and you're generally reaching the end of your tether, don't scream. Call for help.

In addition to the county agencies described elsewhere in this chapter, there are scores of counseling services in the metropolitan area. A number serve special groups, such as parents of children with birth defects, or individuals suffering from specific diseases, or families of alcoholics. But others deal with problems arising in everyday life.

A complete listing of all these organizations is beyond the scope of this book. For detailed information about counseling services and all types of human service agencies, especially those serving the handicapped, contact The United Way (tel.: 522-0110), or consult the United Way's *The Help Book*.

Here we present a very restricted list of agencies providing marital and family counseling to parents and children.

Agency	Fee	Telephone
Catholic Social Services 680 W. Peachtree St., N.W. Atlanta, Ga. 30308	Sliding Scale	881-6571
Family Outreach Center 120 Copeland Rd., N.W., Suite 264 Atlanta, Ga. 30342	Sliding Scale	255-3604

Jewish Family & Children's Bureau Sliding Scale   873-2277
Atlanta Jewish Welfare Federation
1753 Peachtree Rd., N.E.
Atlanta, Ga. 30309

The Bridge   Sliding Scale   881-8344
77 Peachtree Pl., N.W.
Atlanta, Ga. 30309

The Hub   Sliding Scale   934-5600
5115 LaVista Rd.,
Tucker, Ga. 30384

The Link   Sliding Scale   256-9797
218 Hilderbrand Dr., N.E.
Atlanta, Ga. 30328

Hotlines
For Help

24-hour crisis counseling

Agency	Telephone
Fulton County	572-2626
DeKalb County	892-4646
Cobb County	422-0202
Clayton County	996-4357
Gwinnett/Rockdale/Newton Counties	963-3223

24-hour Runaway line, Atlanta

The Bridge/ Salvation Army Girls' Lodge/ Truck Stop Youth Lodge	881-8346

This service can be used by runaway girls and boys who need a place to sleep or someone to talk to. It is supported through funds provided under the National Runaway Youth Act.

National Runaway Lines

National Runaway Switchboard (Chicago)	1-800-621-4000
Peace of Mind (Texas)	1-800-231-6946

**24-hour Emergency Contact With
Americans Abroad**

Emergency Services Center   1-202-632-5225
Washington, D.C.

This line is operated by the U.S. Department of State, Bureau of Consular Affairs.

Rape Crisis Center, 24-hour assistance

Grady Memorial Hospital   659-7273

Poison Control Center

Grady Hospital   588-4400

XIV

TRUE BELIEVERS

Monastery of the Holy Spirit

THAT
OLD TIME
RELIGION

People coming to live in Atlanta from other parts of the country are sometimes taken aback to discover how much it is part of the Bible Belt. It is a city in which churches are filled each Sunday, and new ones are built every year.

In Atlanta, the church regulates not only religion, but also a good part of communal life. On buses, it is not uncommon to see riders engrossed in their Bibles or other religious material. Businessmen like to include the church office they hold in their resumes.

The largest Christian denomination in Atlanta is the Southern Baptist, but most other denominations are also represented here. Atlanta has a fairly large Jewish population as well.

Because of its unique regionalism the Southern Baptist faith is often an enigma to newcomers from other parts of the country and the world. Here is an outline of its main characteristics.

Who Are the Southern Baptists?

The Civil War that separated state from state also caused division within the church. Members of the same denomination went their separate ways in North and South. But after the War, most reunited. Two exceptions were the Southern Baptists and Presbyterians. Both groups elected to retain their independence after peace had been restored.

The Baptists in the South, who outnumbered their Northern brethren, tended to be more conservative in religious and political outlook. According to John B. Hayes, Associate Professor of Old Testament at Emory University's Candler School of Theology, three fundamental principles characterize their beliefs.

The first is the belief that a person must choose to become a member of the Church, rather than simply be born into it. The "born again" experience which some adults undergo is a reflection of this conviction, a voluntary acceptance of Christ.

The second strong feature of the Southern Baptist church is the autonomy of individual congregations within the church. Although a Southern Baptist Convention is held each year, its decisions are not binding on member churches. There is no hierarchy within the church. Each congregation selects its own minister, presumably to reflect its views, and makes its own decisions. In fact, according to Dr. Hayes, only about half the Southern Baptist ministers have had theological training; the rest have merely studied the Bible and found a congregation willing to accept their interpretation of it.

The third principle of the Baptist faith is emphasis on the Bible as the sole authority on matters of faith and ethics. This principle is carried furthest by the "fundamentalist" Baptist sects such as Primitive Baptist congregations.

The result of the autonomy enjoyed by individual churches is that they offer considerable variety. The philosophies they endorse range from relatively liberal to very conservative. In fact, so great is the variation among pastors and churches, that it is common for individuals to shop around until they find a church and pastor whose philosophy they feel comfortable with, and wish to join.

The Black Churches of Atlanta

In Atlanta's earliest days, churches were not segregated. Blacks were admitted as members, usually seated at different times, according to Rev. E. R. Carter's 1894 account, *The Black Side.* Shortly before the Civil War, however, an independent Black church was established. This was the well-known Big Bethel Church, affiliated with the African Methodist Episcopal denomination. Other historic Black churches in Atlanta include the Wheat Street and Ebenezer Baptist churches. Ebenezer is renowned for the fact that Dr. Martin Luther King, Jr. served as pastor there. Another prominent church is First Congregational, which is patronized by many of Atlanta's old Black families.

From the beginning, many of these churches were called on to meet more than just the spiritual needs of their members, according to Dr. James M. Shopshire, professor of the sociology of religion at Atlanta University's Inter-denominational Theological Center. In the absence of other institutions catering to the needs of the Black population, the churches were required to provide education, insurance, and economic assistance for the Black community. Some of Atlanta's biggest modern day Black commercial enterprises, such as the Atlanta Life Insurance Company, started out as church-operated aid societies.

Though the economic function of the Black church has diminished in importance, the role of the church as a unifying cultural force survives. It was also out of the churches that much of the leadership of the Black community evolved, including, in recent times, Dr. King and Andrew Young.

Atlanta's Black churches conform generally to the same denominational groupings and hierarchical structure as the White churches. The Baptists have the largest following, with the Methodists running second. There are also a number of charismatic Pentecostal churches, as well as several churches which reinterpret Christianity in the light of the Black experience.

Best known of the churches in the last category is the Shrine of the Black Madonna. It was founded in Detroit by Rev. Albert Cleage. The church's basic doctrines are Christian, but they have been adapted to reflect a form of Black cultural nationalism. The church's Atlanta headquarters are at 944 Gordon Street, S.W., and also include a cultural center, a gallery with African artifacts, an art gallery, and a bookstore.

The Pentecostal churches originated in the lower Mississippi valley, according to Dr. Shopshire. They evolved out of the missionary Baptist churches, and spread very rapidly. The biggest of the Black Pentecostal churches in Atlanta is the Church of God in Christ; there are also a number of White Pentecostal churches in the region.

The Pentecostal churches are evangelic and frequently charismatic. The key to their services is evidence of the presence of the Holy Spirit as shown through the Nine Gifts of God. The best known of these are the gift of speaking in tongues, and the gift of interpretation. Speaking in tongues is the gift of speaking, under the influence of the spirit, in a language not intelligible except to those who possess the gift of interpretation. Another evidence of the working of the spirit is offered when members of the congregation begin the "prayer dance."

Atlanta, in short, offers hospitable soil for most forms of belief except agnosticism or atheism.

The Great

"To live as a monk is a great gift, not given to many."
——Thomas Merton

Once it was out in the country near Conyers. Now housing and commercial developments are creeping up to its boundaries. But tranquility still pervades the atmosphere of the Monastery of the Holy Spirit.

Not perhaps at the bustling gatehouse where the monks sell their homebaked bread and the produce of their brother monasteries. But serenity reigns in the secluded cloister, the cool quiet of the abbey chapel where light filtering blue through narrow windows highlights the austere simplicity of modern Gothic, and on the shores of the small lake where white swans glide with eyes watchful for crumbs.

The Cistercian monks who founded the abbey came to Conyers in 1944 from their parent monastery of Gethsemani, near Louisville, Kentucky. During the next 20 years, they built the abbey with their own hands, manual labor being regarded as a form of prayer.

The monks who enter the Monastery of the Holy Spirit take vows of obedience, stability and conversion of life. Their day begins at 2:15 am with prayer. Prayer, meditation and labor alternate

Gift

throughout the day until they retire at 7 pm. As Trappists, they refrain from unnecessary talk, using signals where possible to take the place of speech.

The abbey's monks maintain their independence from the world by doing business with it. In order to be self-supporting, they raise cattle, grow and sell hay, operate a nursery, market their Monastery Bread, create works in stained glass for other churches, and make a variety of crafts.

The peace of the monastery is not withheld from others. The Monastery has a guest-house where men who wish to make a retreat from the world can stay for a few days. The abbey church and grounds are also open to visitors; only men may enter the cloisters.

You may feel, as Gerald Manley Hopkins wrote of a nun taking the veil, that you have arrived

> *Where no storms come,*
> *Where the green swell is in the havens dumb,*
> *And out of the swing of the sea.*

To reach the Monastery, take I-20 E to the second Conyers exit (Ga. 138). Turn right (south) on Ga. 138, then left on Ga. 212. The abbey will be on your left off Ga. 212.

DENOMINATIONS

To gain some idea of the almost bewildering variety of Christian denominations represented in Atlanta it is necessary only to look at the Yellow Pages under the heading "Churches." They run the gamut from the most established creeds, such as Methodist, Catholic, and Episcopalian, to sects such as "Bible," "Gospel Harvester," Mennonite, "Open Bible," and "Religious Science" churches. Non-Christian sects such as Baha'i, Hare Krishna, the Divine Light mission, and others are also present in the city.

There are nine Jewish synagogues in Atlanta, both orthodox and reformed, and there is a small Hasidic community in the city as well. The Jewish Community Center publishes a newcomer's kit that provides a good deal of information about matters of interest to the Jewish community.

Here's a list of organizations representing some of the larger religious denominations in Atlanta.

Denomination	Telephone
A.M.E. Church Headquarters, 208 Auburn Ave., N.E.	659-2012
Atlanta Jewish Community Center 1745 Peachtree Rd., N.E.	875-7881
C.M.E. Church Headquarters, 2001 M.L. King Jr. Dr., S.W.	752-7800
Catholic Archdiocese of Atlanta, 680 W. Peachtree St., N.W.	881-6441

Christian Council of Metropolitan Atlanta, 881-9890
848 Peachtree St., N.E.

Church of God State Offices (Pentecostal), 448-9300
6179 Buford Hwy.,
Doraville.

Episcopal Diocese of Atlanta, 261-3791
2744 Peachtree Rd., N.W.

Christian Science Church, 233-1305
3230 Peachtree Rd., N.E.

Atlanta Baptist Association, 874-5206
1370 Spring St., N.W.

Greek Orthodox Cathedral of the Annunciation, 633-5870
2500 Clairmont Rd., N.E.

Presbyterian Center, 873-1531
341 Ponce de Leon Ave., N.E.

United Presbyterian Synod of the South, 768-4436
1001 Virginia Ave.,
Hapeville.

Southeastern Synod of the Lutheran Churches of America, 873-1977
756 W. Peachtree St., N.E.

Southern Union Conference of Seventh-Day Adventists, 299-1832
3978 Memorial Dr.,
Decatur.

Unitarian Universalist Congregation of Atlanta, 634-5134
1911 Cliff Valley Way, N.E.

United Methodist Church Headquarters, 659-6611
159 Ralph McGill Blvd., N.E.

The Church
Of The Deaf

From the outside, the small, square structure looks more like a warehouse than a house of worship. But inside is a church that is unique in the Southeast, and one of only five in the nation: a church wholly owned and managed by the deaf and for the deaf. This church is the Crusselle-Freeman Church of the Deaf, located at 1304 Allene Avenue, S. W.

A close sense of community and companionship among its congregation is its chief feature. It's a church that tries to serve as many deaf people as possible. So its worship is non-denominational, its membership non-racial and of all ages, and its services conducted in sign language with a spoken translation, to reach both deaf parents and their hearing children.

Like any other church, Crusselle-Freeman has a Sunday school. And a choir: a deaf choir. Conducted by a hearing person who gives the rhythm, the choir interprets hymns in a carefully choreographed symphony of signs. At Christmas, in a darkened church, and wearing black gowns, the choir sings carols with white-gloved hands, so that the joyous signs ripple from one end of the dais to the other.